1985

The Delicacy and Strength of Lace

THE DELICACY AND STRENGTH OF LACE

Letters between

LESLIE MARMON SILKO

&

JAMES WRIGHT

Edited and with an introduction by Anne Wright

GRAYWOLF PRESS • SAINT PAUL

The illustration originally accompanied an
excerpt from this book in *Milkweed Chronicle*,
Vol. 6, No. 3.

"The Lace" by Rainer Maria Rilke, translated
by Franz Wright, is used by permission of
Field magazine.

ISBN 0-915308-74-6
Library of Congress Catalog card number 85-80977

Published by Graywolf Press
2402 University Avenue
Suite 203
Saint Paul, Minnesota 55114

4 6 8 9 7 5

INTRODUCTION

Leslie Silko and James Wright met only twice. The delicacy and strength of their friendship was to grow through letters.

They first met, briefly, in the summer of 1975 at a writers conference in Michigan. Three years later, while on holiday in Rhode Island, James read *Ceremony* and began their correspondence with a short note of praise for the book. The formality of their first few letters was broken when Leslie began to relate stories about a tyrannical black rooster that lived on her ranch. Soon they were exchanging work, discussing the difficulties of writing when "besieged by personal turmoil" and the rewards when it went well.

While on a year's leave of absence in Europe, James wrote from Albi, France, "I was so happy to hear from you. We must keep faithfully in touch." Back in Arizona, Leslie was to respond in kind, "I deeply appreciate your letters and cards – it is as if they bring me along with you and Annie in your travels."

An invitation to speak at the University of Arizona in the spring of 1980 seemed to promise a time when they would "certainly meet and have good long walks and talks," when Leslie could "point out the little I have learned to recognize here."

It was not to happen. In January of 1980 James entered Mount Sinai Hospital with terminal cancer. Their second and final meeting was in a hospital room. Leslie Silko ended her last letter to James Wright saying: "...no matter if written words are seldom, because we know, Jim, we know."

Anne Wright
New York City

THE LACE

1

Being human: term for a flickering possession,
existence of a happiness still undemonstrated:
is it inhuman, that a pair of eyes
turned into this small densely woven piece of lace?
Do you want them back?

You, long since vanished, and finally blind –
is all your human joy here inside this thing
where your huge feelings went, as between
stem and bark, miniaturized?

Through a tear in fate, a tiny interstice,
you absented your soul from its own time;
and it is so present here in this light
section of lace, it makes me smile at "usefulness."

2

And if someday all we have done
and all that has happened to us
seems so inferior and strange,
as though there'd been no point
in taking the trouble to outgrow our first pair of shoes
just to come to this – ...Shouldn't this
strip of yellowed lace, this tightly meshed
flowery border of lace suffice
to keep us here? Look: this at least got *done.*

A life was ignored in the process, who knows.
A delight was there, was going to be sacrificed,
and finally at any cost
there would exist this thing, not easier than life
yet *finished* and so lovely, as though it weren't too soon
to smile and soar.

Rainer Maria Rilke
translated by Franz Wright

The Delicacy and Strength of Lace

Misquamicut
Rhode Island
August 28, 1978

Dear Mrs. Silko,

I trust you won't mind hearing from a stranger. Not entirely a stranger though. About three summers ago I heard you read some stories and poems at that national poetry conference in Michigan. At that time I realized, like everybody else who was present, that your reading brought us all into the presence of something truly remarkable. Since then, I've read your work in some anthologies, always with the same feeling.

Now I have finally had the chance to read *Ceremony*, and I am moved to tell you how much the book means to me. In some strange way it seems inadequate to call it a great book, though it is surely that, or a perfect work of art, though it is one. I could call *Ceremony* one of the four or five best books I have ever read about America and I would be speaking the truth. But even this doesn't say just what I mean.

I think I am trying to say that my very life means more to me than it would have meant if you hadn't written *Ceremony*. But this sounds inadequate also.

It was a very great thing to meet you, however briefly, in Michigan, and I am very happy that you are alive and writing books.

Sincerely,
James Wright

❦

Tucson, Arizona
September 9, 1978

Dear Mr. Wright,

Your letter came at a time when I needed it most. So many sad things have happened with my marriage and my children – it is good to know that my work means something.

I remember you well from the Michigan time – because you had been ill and you reminded me of my grandfather though I know you are a much younger man – grandfather in the sense that I grew up with. I remember the poems you read – new ones you said, and I remember still your voice. I'm not sure if I could find you by your face. It was those "new ones" that moved me – some sheer tenacity in them and no frills of "style" (I feel so much an outsider and alien to mainstream poetic style). Your directness and leanness I could understand in the way that the old people at home talked. I don't know the world of poetry that most American writers my age know. I know Shakespeare's histories but I know so little of Pound or even Lowell. But when I heard you I thought well maybe academic background only runs so far, and then finally it is simple guts and heart.

I don't know if this expresses the importance of your letter for me. Probably not. But I want you to know that writing it had made a great difference for me, and I wish to thank you.

Sincerely,
Leslie Silko

❦

Newark, Delaware
September 25, 1978

Dear Mrs. Silko,

I treasure the beauty of your letter, and I venture to hope that you will write again, even a note. There is something very important about keeping in touch, however briefly.

I just wrote and asked my editor at Farrar, Straus and Giroux, in New York, to send you my new book. It is called *To a Blossoming Pear Tree*. I would send it directly from here, but I don't have but one copy, already somewhat worn. The book contains the "new work" that you mentioned, and some other pieces.

May I ask if you've published any collections of your poems? The ones that rise out of the text are very beautiful even when taken by themselves, and I have read others. I think it is astonishing to see your mastery of the novel combined with a power of poetry within it.

I want to make a suggestion, if I may. Have you ever applied for a Guggenheim Fellowship? Conceivably – please don't take my word for it – it may be a little late to apply for this year, but, even so, it wouldn't hurt to get the forms from them anyway, for next year.

I want to confess something to you, something that distresses me: a few weeks ago I had a note from Dr. Ray, who asked me to recommend somebody for the Guggenheim Fellowship, so he could send the forms. Blind idiot that I am, I didn't think to send your name. Still, if you should try for next year, I would feel honored if you would write down my name to write a letter of recommendation for you. I'm afraid I'm sounding awfully pompous making this suggestion. Still, I'm following a hunch.

I want to get this note in the mail now. I would be happy to hear from you again.

In friendship,
James Wright

Tucson, Arizona
October 3, 1978

Dear Mr. Wright,
Dear Jim,

I just fed the rooster a blackened banana I found in the refrigerator. He has been losing his yellowish collar feathers lately, and I'm afraid it might be that he isn't getting enough to eat. But I suppose it could be his meanness too – he is the rooster out of all the rooster stories my grandmother ever told me – the rooster who waited inside the barn on winter mornings when it was still dark and my grandma was just married and going to milk her father-in-law's cow. The rooster would wait and ambush her just when she thought she had escaped him. It was a reflexive reaction the morning he jumped to rake her with his spurs and she swung the milking bucket at him. He collapsed and didn't move, and the whole time she was milking the cow she wondered how she could ever tell her father-in-law, my great-grandfather, that she had killed his rooster. She took the milk inside and he was already drinking his coffee. (He was an old man by then, the old white man who came from Ohio and married my great-grandmother from Paguate village north of Laguna.) She told him she didn't mean to kill the rooster but that the bucket hit him too hard. They tell me that my great-grandfather was a gentle person. And Grandma said that morning he told her not to worry, that he had known for a while that rooster was too mean to keep. But as they went out to the barn together, to dispose of the dead rooster, there he was in the corral. Too mean to kill, Grandma said. But after that, he left her alone when she went to milk the cow.

There are all kinds of other rooster stories that one is apt to hear. I am glad I have this rooster because I never quite believed roosters so consistently *were* as the stories tell us they are. On these hot Tucson days, he scatches a little nest in the damp dirt under the Mexican lime tree by the front door. It is imperative for him that the kittens and the black cat show him respect, even deference, by detouring or half-circling the rooster as they approach the water dish which is also under the lime tree. If they fail to do this, then he jumps up and stamps his feet, moving sideways until they cringe. This done, he goes back to his mud nest.

He has all of us fooled, stepping around him softly, hesitant to turn our backs on him, all of us except for the old black hound dog. She won't let anyone, including the rooster, come between her and her food dish. The rooster pretends he does not notice her lack of concern; he pretends he was just finished eating when she approaches.

The lady at the feed store had to give him away. He was her pet and he let her pick him up and stroke him. But the men who came to buy hay got to teasing him and he started going after all the feed store customers. She was afraid he might hurt a child. So I took him and told her I didn't know how long he'd last here at the ranch because the coyotes are everywhere in the Tucson mountains. I didn't expect him to last even a week. But that was in June and now it is October. Maybe it is his meanness after all that keeps the coyotes away, that makes his feathers fall out.

I never know what will happen when I write a letter. Certain persons bring out certain things in me. I hadn't intended to go off with rooster stories when really I wanted to tell you how happy I was to hear from you again. I am very much looking forward to your new book. I am sort of hungry for contact with poetry again. I think it must have been all the emotional upheaval that turned me away from books, from reading. I called it futility and too few poems which can speak anymore. But I think I was the one who couldn't hear very well. It helps, too, to look in the right places. I wasn't searching for the books.

I was only reading the poetry that happened to come my way – a book here, a magazine there. I have to guard against my tendency to feel like I am an outsider, that I don't belong to the current American writing scene. Maybe the less contact I have with the poetry and writing, the less I am reminded of how I don't quite fit in. But I trust your voice, just as I trust a few others. And it is time I turn to you whom I trust, to listen and to find out what you have been discovering while I sat with my fingers in my ears.

I am enclosing the little book that was done in 1974, and some xeroxes of subsequent pieces.* I'm not a terribly prolific writer. I write only a few poems when I am involved in a fiction project. Lately, I am reworking old-time Laguna narratives into experimental film scripts, and this project has cut into my time for other writing. (Actually it *isn't* the scripts, it is the rest of the mess – divorce, money, etc. – that has interfered, not the scripts. I love the scripts.) Anyway, until I get the collection together for Viking (a collection of poetry and short fiction) this is all that I have to share with you.

Thank you for encouraging me to apply for a Guggenheim. I had the forms (I order them every year but then never have the courage to submit them) and so now I will finally do it.

I am relieved to hear that your health has been good. I can appreciate what illness can do to one's life. A year ago, this month, I had to undergo emergency abdominal surgery. Before the internal bleeding was discovered, I was unable to concentrate. I thought I was losing my mind. As it turns out I was only two pints short of blood – enough to slow my brain down. Anyway, let us both continue to feel well, and to persist.

I hope this letter doesn't seem out of place. Probably the next time I write to you I won't launch into stories or mono-

*The little book was *Laguna Woman.* There was also a xerox of "Storyteller" and the following poems.

logues on my reading habits. Usually I write letters about broken pumps or windmills here or even about how my car isn't running so well. But today I could not stop myself. I think I must have been wanting to write about the roosters for a long time. Usually I don't write long letters, and I don't want you to feel like you have to answer in kind or anything like that. But I would like to stay in touch with you.

Sincerely,
Leslie

❀

Tucson, Arizona

Dear Jim,

These are only a few of the pieces done since '73 and the *Laguna Woman* book. I will send you others as I find them or xerox them.

Apologies,
Leslie

❀

Note on the Deer Dance:

In the fall the Laguna hunters go to the hills and mountains around Laguna Pueblo to bring back the deer. The people think of the deer as coming to give themselves to the hunters so that the people will have meat through the winter. Late in the winter the Deer Dance is performed to honor and pay thanks to the deer spirits who've come home with the hunters that year. Only when this has been properly done will the spirits be able to return to the mountain and be reborn into more deer who will, remembering the reverence and appreciation of the people, once more come home with the hunters.

If this
will hasten your return
then I will hold myself above you all night
blowing softly
down-feathered clouds
that drift above the spruce
and hide your eyes
as you are borne back
to the mountain.

Years ago
through the yellow oak leaves
antlers polished like stones
in the canyon stream-crossing.
    Morning turned in the sky
    when I saw you
    and I wanted the gift
    you carry on moon-color shoulders
    so big
    the size of you
    holds the long winter.

You have come home with me before
a long way down the mountain.
The people welcome you.
I took
the best red blanket for you
the turquoise the silver rings
were very old

something familiar for you
blue corn meal saved special.

While others are sleeping
I tie feathers on antlers
whisper close to you
we have missed you
I have longed for you.

Losses are certain
in the pattern of this dance.
Over the terrain a hunter travels
blind curves in the trail
seize the breath
until it leaps away
loose again
to run the hills.
Go quickly.

How beautiful
this last time
I touch you
to believe
and hasten the return
of lava-slope hills and
your next-year heart

Mine still beats
in the tall grass
where you stopped.
Go quickly.

Year by year
after the first snowfall

I will walk these hills and
    pray you will come again
I will go with a heart full for you
    to wait your return.

The neck pulse slacks,
then smooths.
It has been a long time.
Sundown forms change.
Faces are unfamiliar
    as the last warmth goes
    from under my hand.
    Hooves scatter rocks
    down the hillside
    and I turn to you
The run
for the length of the mountain
is only beginning.

STORY FROM BEAR COUNTRY

You will know
when you walk
in bear country.
By the silence
flowing swiftly between juniper trees
by the sundown colors of sandrock
all around you.

You may smell damp earth
scratched away
from yucca roots.
You may hear snorts and growls

slow and massive sounds
from caves
in the cliffs high above you.

It is difficult to explain
how they call you.
All but a few who went to them
left behind families
        grandparents
        and sons
        a good life.

The problem is
you will never want to return.
Their beauty will overcome your memory
like winter sun
melting ice shadows from snow.
And you will remain with them
locked forever inside yourself
        your eyes will see you
        dark shaggy thick.

We can send bear priests
loping after you
their medicine bags
bouncing against their chests.
Naked legs painted black
bear claw necklaces
rattling against
their capes of blue spruce.

They will follow your trail
into the narrow canyon
through the blue-gray mountain sage

to the clearing
where you stopped to look back
and saw only bear tracks
behind you.

When they call
faint memories
will writhe around your heart
and startle you with their distance.
But the others will listen
because bear priests sing
beautiful songs.
They must
if they are ever to call you back.

They will try to bring you
step by step
back to the place you stopped
and found only bear prints in the sand
where your feet had been.

Whose voice is this?
You may wonder
hearing this story when
after all
you are alone
hiking in these canyons and hills
while your wife and sons are waiting
back at the car for you.

But you have been listening to me
for some time now
from the very beginning in fact
and you are alone in this canyon of stillness

not even cedar birds flutter.
See, the sun is going down now
the sandrock is washed in its colors.
Don't be afraid
        we love you
        we've been calling you
all this time.
Go ahead
turn around
see the shape
of your footprints
in the sand.

24 July 1975
Ketchikan

from OUT OF THE WORKS NO GOOD COMES FROM

Incantation

The television
lights the room,
a continual presence.
Seconds minutes
flicker in gray intervals
on the wall beside my head.
Even if
I could walk to the window
I would only see
gray video images
bending against the clouds.

At one time
more might have been necessary –
    a smoky quartz crystal
    balanced in the center of the palm.
But tonight
there is enough.

The simple equation you found
in my notebook
frightened you.
But I could have explained it:
    After all bright colors of sunset and leaf
    are added together
    lovers are subtracted
    children multiplied, divided, taken away.
The remainder is small enough
to stay in this room forever
gray-shadowing restless
trapped on a gray glass plain.

I did not plan to tell you.
Better to lose colors gradually
first the blue of the eyes
then the red of blood
its salt taste fading
water gone suddenly bitter
when the last yellow light
blinks off the screen.

Wherever you're heading tonight
you think you're leaving me
    and the equation of this gray room.
Hold her close
    pray

these are lies I'm telling you.
As with the set which lost its color
and only hums gray outlines
it is a matter of intensity and hue
and the increasing distance –
the interval will grow as imperceptibly
as it grew between us.

You'll drive on
putting distance and time between us
the snow in the high Sierras
the dawn along the Pacific
dreaming you've left this narrow room.

But tonight
I have traced all escape routes
with my finger across the T.V. weather map.
Your ocean dawn is only the gray light
in the corner of this room.
Your mountain snowstorm
flies against the glass screen
until we both are buried.

SKELETON FIXER'S STORY*

What happened here?
she asked
Some kind of accident?

*A piece from *A Bigger Story They Tell Around Laguna and Acoma* (from a version told by Simon J. Ortiz).

Words like bones.
Scattered all over the place...

Old Man Badger traveled
from place to place
searching for skeleton bones.
There was something
only he could do with them.

On the smooth sand
Old Man Badger started laying out the bones.
It was a great puzzle for him.
He started with the toes.
He loved their curve
like a new moon,
like a white whisker hair.

Without thinking
he knew their direction,
laying each toe bone
to walk east.

"I know,
it must have been this way.
Yes,"
he talked to himself while he worked.

He strung the spine bones
as beautiful as any shell necklace.

The leg bones were running
so fast
dust from the ankle joints
surrounded the wind.

"Oh poor dear one who left your bones here
I wonder who you are?"
Old Skeleton Fixer spoke to the bones
because things don't die –
they fall to pieces maybe,
get scattered or separate,
but Old Badger Man can tell
how they once fit together.

Though he didn't recognize the bones
he could not stop;
he loved them anyway.

He took great care with the ribs
marveling at the structure
which had contained the lungs and heart.
Skeleton Fixer had never heard of
such things as souls.
He was certain
only of bones.

But where a heart once beat
there was only sand.
"Oh I will find you one –
somewhere around here!"
And a yellow butterfly
flew up from the grass at his feet.

"Ah I know how your breath left you –
like butterflies over an edge,
not falling but fluttering
their wings rainbow colors.
Wherever they are
your heart will be."

He worked all day
He was so careful with this one –
it felt like the most special of all.
Old Badger Man didn't stop
until the last spine bone
was arranged at the base of the tail.

"A'moo'ooh, my dear one
these words are your bones,"
he repeated this
four times

"pa pa pa pa!
pa pa pa pa!
pa pa pa pa!
pa pa pa pa!"

Old Coyote Woman jumped up
and took off running.
She never even said "thanks."

Skeleton Fixer
shook his head slowly.

"It is surprising sometimes,"
he said,
"how these things turn out."

But he never has stopped fixing
the poor scattered bones he finds.

Newark, Delaware
October 12, 1978

Dear Leslie,

Some years ago – I forget how many – a friend wrote me a note from Chicago. I call him my friend, though at the time I hadn't met him. His note was simple: "I'm so lonely I can't stand it. I don't mean solitude. I need solitude. But loneliness rots the soul." It sounds as if I were just making this up, but I swear that's what he wrote to me, and all he wrote to me. My response will sound improbable and "literary" too, I'm afraid. Nevertheless, it is the simple truth: I immediately wrote to him that I was going to find him in Chicago on the day after Thanksgiving (I wonder what year it was) and that, furthermore, I was going to bring with me two pretty girls and a bunch of bananas.

I did it too. I forget how I did it, but I did it. We spent a long weekend, talking and shooting pool. Then I went back to St. Paul, Minnesota, where I was living at the time.

I've been thinking about his remarks about loneliness and solitude, because I am closer to finding the proper ceremony for my life now. I hope you'll forgive me for appropriating that word "ceremony" but it is a true word, and I need it. My ceremony is to rise early. It is in the early hours that I feel most at home with myself. My wife Annie doesn't rise so early, and I sit for a couple of hours pondering things. During the past week...the past four days, I should say...I've been spending those hours with your stories and poems. It's curious that I've thought about them throughout the day, and felt eager to return to them the next morning. I've had the poems with me in my briefcase, and even now, when I'm in my office and pondering what I'm going to say to my students this afternoon and how I'm going to try to listen to them, I've just gone through *Laguna Woman* yet again. It is curious how such a brief book has such enormous space in it, a space full of echoes and voices.

Of course your long letter gave me the same sense of something inexhaustible and refreshing. It made me happy, not only because of the story about the rooster, but because the very prose of the letter embodied, with its clarity and speed and force, that same spirit that moved with such ease and great strength through *Ceremony*, the novel. I think the word I am looking for is "abundance." You are abundant. I don't mean cluttered or overgrown. Abundant, rather, as the seasons themselves are abundant. Again, I may be sounding "literary" and that would be a pity, because I am trying to find words here for something that is very real for me. I am extremely glad, and, in a way, *relieved*, that you exist.

I once endured a divorce. I mention this, not to tell you the story of my life, which is commonplace and boring, but only to suggest that I can understand how bruised, even shattered, you have felt. And the poems make it clear how deep and painful the bruises are. Well, as you say, we must persist, and take heart. As you wrote with something like absolute finality in "Storyteller," it is essential that the story be told, and that someone go on telling it. I don't think it's mere flattery to tell you that no living writer known to me so deeply grasps that truth, and its significance, as you do. I know I need that truth, and your clarification of it, and I am very far from being the only one.

It makes me feel slightly formal to tell you that I am from Ohio. My family goes very far and very deep back into Ohio and West Virginia.

Let me tell you what is up here. I am here at Delaware as a visiting professor for the Fall semester. Annie and I hope to be in Paris before Christmas, and we want to spend that holiday in Chartres. Then we will be in Europe for eight months, much of the time in beloved Italy, in Apulia, the heel of the boot. As soon as we type up our itinerary, I'll send it to you, and I hope we can continue to keep in touch, even during the wanderings.

Please write when you can, even briefly.

When you refer in your poems to "Mei"* is she by chance the Chinese-American girl who was also out in Michigan? If so, I've met her again, at Galway Kinnell's house. She is a fine person indeed, and also a beautiful poet.

You've sent me back to my own notebook, and I had a slow and lovely time this morning with a short poem. It takes me forever to get anything done, but sometimes I do.

With friendship
always,
Jim

❦

Tucson, Arizona
October 17, 1978

Dear Jim,

I'm reading the poems slowly, a few each day, some again and again. I try not to have "favorites" (the way a parent tries to love all the children the same) but I always believed in love at first sight with poetry if not people and places. So I read the favorites again and again while exploring the new pieces. I love "Verona in the Rain" and "The Wheeling Gospel Tabernacle" and "The Shell of a Hermit Crab" and "In Exile." I'm moving slowly, so I haven't found all that I know I will love. By love I mean that I embrace the poems without any particulars on form, structure and style all those things that people are supposed to think about when they read poetry (or write it, for that matter). I read them the way I write them: by feeling my

*See *Laguna Woman*.

way to them. Then I find certain lines that I could live with forever:

> "Even the noon sunlight in the Colosseum is the
> golden shadow of a starved lion, the most beautiful
> of God's creatures except maybe horses."
>
> *and*
>
> "But they will last long enough. I would rather live
> my life than not live it. The grapes in a smallish stall
> are as huge and purple as smoke. I have just eaten one.
> I have eaten the first fruit of the season, and I am in
> love."

I love the repetition of "for all I know" in "Wheeling Gospel." The storyteller at Laguna uses the repetition and also the teller's refusal to take credit for knowing anything for sure although *we* feel sure of the truth in the telling.

I am pushing to finish the first of the scripts which attempt to tell the Laguna stories on film using the storyteller's voice with the actual locations where these stories are supposed to have taken place. In a strange sort of way, the film project is an experiment in translation – bringing the land – the hills, the arroyos, the boulders, the cottonwoods in October – to people unfamiliar with it, because after all, the stories grow out of this land as much as we see ourselves as having emerged from the land there. Translations of Laguna stories seem terribly bleak on the printed page. A voice, a face, hands to point and gesture bring them alive, but if you do not know the places which the storyteller calls up in the telling, if you have not waded in the San Jose River below the village, if you have not hidden in the river willows and sand with your lover, then even as the teller relates a story, you will miss something which people from the Laguna community would not have missed. Laguna narratives are very lean because so much of the stories are shared knowledge – certainly descriptions of the river and the river willows are *not* included in the narratives because it is assumed the listeners already know the river and the willows. So with a wonderful cinematographer, I hope to bring the stories out in a manner most faithful to the heart of the Laguna storyteller. Film will be used to create a context, a place within which the narratives reside. It is all an experiment and film is such a complex and expensive medium. We will be lucky to ever see it on film. But the texts of the stories are beautiful and the visualization in the script is beautiful too, so I already feel that whatever the outcome, I will have written something interesting. I needed to wean myself from involved descriptions of the land, and the script has helped. I think I am learning something, too, about possibilities as well as the limits of visual imagery and verbal images. I am continually surprised at the things we writers think nothing of attempting with language – things which are impossible visually. On the other hand, film images can be strung together and the viewer's mind associates them in a way which dispenses with the "bridges" and "transitions" which writers must deal with.

Well, I hope this isn't too tedious – this discussion of visual and verbal, etc. I like to keep learning and this is one of my more ambitious undertakings.

The rooster is growing new feathers. The mares are fat but their hooves are dried-out from lack of rain and they shatter (This makes it sound worse than it really is. The old parts of the hoof break off and they lose their horseshoes.) when we ride over the rocks too fast. The coyotes haven't eaten the kittens yet, but one of the kittens tried to climb a cholla cactus yesterday and I spent the afternoon pulling cactus spines out of her belly, tail and paws.

Thank you again for sending *To a Blossoming Pear Tree* – it is a powerful book for me.

Sincerely,
Leslie

Newark, Delaware
October 28, 1978

Dear Leslie,

It is thrilling to read your words about the scripts you are working on, and I can well understand what you mean by the stories depending in part on shared knowledge, so that, in the telling alone, the proper audience can grasp the references and fill in the landscapes. But I wonder if I can tell you something that has occurred to me, and not only in the present context. To write out of, and with, a shared context implies a proper, knowledgable audience. It occurs to me that, just as you say, with the right cinematographer you can create the audience which will share the knowledge of the story. That is beautiful and true. But at one point in your discussion, you say, "I need to wean myself from involved descriptions of the land...." I trust you are referring to your actual work on the scripts, and not at all to your descriptions of the landscape in your fiction. For it is just those descriptions that, in the novel, and the stories, do so much to create the stories that you are telling there. I did not feel that your descriptions of landscape were merely ornamental or in any way superfluous. On the contrary, one of the many great strengths to be felt in *Ceremony*, for example, is your ability to describe beyond description, so to speak – your way of dealing with landscape there is not just a point up of details, but the evocation (I can't think of a better word) of something – a spirit perhaps? Anyway, the effect is, for me, that of almost hearing the landscape itself tell the story.

These are just occasional thoughts in response to your words about the scripts. What you say is far from "tedious" – it's exciting.

You made me happy with your words about *To a Blossoming Pear Tree*. I think, at bottom, the most one hopes for in writing a book is to find a true response from someone who cares about and genuinely respects....I want to send this note now. Cheers for the recovering rooster.

Love,
Jim

❖

Tucson, Arizona
November 1, 1978

Dear Jim,

Writing to you is a special pleasure I save for myself, just as I look forward to your letters. If my letter has sent you back to your notebook, then your letters have sent me back to scribbles about played-out silver mines and the Grants, New Mexico, Train Robbery of 1918.

Your proposed travels sound very wonderful, and I will be excited to continue our correspondence while you are abroad. I'm not sure if I am a very skillful traveler. Once I went for a month to Bethel, Alaska, an Eskimo town of 2,500, eight miles from the Bering Sea. Each day I spent there, I wanted less to ever leave, and on the 29th day I feared I had changed so that I could never leave the Bethel people without a terrible feeling of loss and sadness, as if I had been born there. It took great effort to leave Bethel, and still I feel I must return there again. Perhaps I am a settler, not a traveler.

You pointed out a very important dimension of the land and the Pueblo people's relation to the land when you said it was as if the land was telling the stories in the novel. That is it exactly, but it is so difficult to convey this interrelationship without sounding like Margaret Fuller or some other Transcendentalist. When I was writing *Ceremony* I was so terribly devastated by being away from the Laguna country that the writing was my way of re-making that place, the Laguna country, for myself. In sand paintings the little geometric forms are said to designate mountains, planets, rainbows – in one sand painting or another all things in Creation are traced out in sand. What I learned for myself was that words can function like the sand. I say "learned for myself" because I think most poets and writers understand this, but it is the kind of lesson that must be found on one's own. I wish I knew Plato better. But didn't he talk about the idea of the tree being more real or important than the actual physical tree itself? Well, I don't exactly agree with *that* either, but I think there is a materialistic impulse in Western thought which says that if you don't have "the real thing – untouched and unchanged" then you don't have anything of value/meaning. When the Army Corps of Engineers flooded the sacred shrines and land near Cochiti Pueblo, many non-Indian people (and Indians as well) said, "Well, it is all ruined. Why do they (the Cochitis) even go near those places?" But here it seems is an instance where this quasi-Platonic idea works well: the strong feelings, the love, the regard which the Cochiti people had for those places that were flooded, those feelings and the importance of those feelings, memories and beliefs are much more important than the physical locations. Which isn't to say that a great hurt and loss didn't occur when the shrines were flooded, but the idea or memory or feeling – whatever you want to call it – is more powerful and important than any damage or destruction humans may commit. How well you know this, express this in your writing – "Lament for the Shadows," "By the Ruins of Gun Emplacement," "One Last Look at the Adige." How much I love this!

It is the same with death. Death never ends feelings or relationships at Laguna. If a dear one passes on, the love continues and it continues in both directions – it is requited by the spirits of these dear ones who send blessings back to us, maybe with rain or maybe with the feeling of continuity and closeness as well as with past memories. And people still speak of old enemies as if the battle continues. For the family it means putting a pinch of food into a bowl for the spirits (family members/relatives) before eating the meal. I'm not sure what Plato would say to this, but here, it seems to me, we have an idea or memory or concept of a person enduring long after the actual, physical person is gone. And so, Jim, here is still another demonstration of the old saying "a little knowledge (of Plato) is dangerous."

Today is All Souls' Day and for both Mexican and Pueblo people it is the day when the dead are especially remembered, but not like Memorial Day exactly. Tonight at Laguna, there will be candles lighting the graves and there will be all kinds of food – favorite dishes like chili stew and roasted piñon nuts – for the souls of loved ones. People try to remember favorite foods of the dead person. At Laguna, when someone dies, you don't "get over it" by forgetting; you "get over it" by *remembering*, and by remembering you are aware that no person is ever truly lost or gone once they have been in our lives and loved us, as we have loved them. Which isn't to say that you conduct life exactly as if the person were alive. If Grandpa didn't like red paint, after he is gone you can feel free to paint the walls red because it is understood that those sorts of things are no longer concerns of the dead.

Navajos and some other tribes don't feel that way, of course – they fear the dead souls. And Eskimos actually name children for dead ancestors with the belief that the soul has returned in that child, though they also realize that this is *not* always the case. So it isn't a *strict* idea of reincarnation like some Asian cultures have.

Howard Rock was a wonderful man who began the first Alaska Native newspaper in Alaska, called the *Tundra Times*. He knew how much the Eskimo and Athabascan people wanted to hear about village news, so he recruited wonderful village correspondents whose use of the English language was unequaled for expressiveness, if a little ungrammatical. Anyway, I used to read his paper while I lived in Ketchikan, and each week he had a little story from childhood in a village near Nome. One week he recalled that when he was 5 years old, his aunt took him ice fishing for grayling. They traveled a distance from the village with their dogs and then she chopped a hole in the ice and they began fishing. This aunt called the boy "Grandmother" because he had been named, at birth, the same name his great-grandmother had had. This day, Howard Rock related, though he was just a little child, he caught many many grayling. And as they were going home that evening his aunt said to him, "Grandmother, you always were the best at ice fishing."

I am reading David Hume so that I understand him a little better than I understand Plato. I have always wondered about Western views of cause and effect vs. Pueblo views of the same. Hume is refreshing. How brave and free of his times he was! How I admire his thinking. He died 200 years ago and even now, most people don't think as freely about cause and effect as he did.

My youngest son visited last week, and it was so wonderful to be with him again. All this personal turmoil takes me from the writing, but I have faith that all these stories inside me will wait. And so I must be patient a little longer.

The rooster has two little white hens now and he is *very proud.*

Love,
Leslie

❁

Newark, Delaware
November 16, 1978

Dear Leslie,

Your last letter was extraordinarily beautiful, as your letters always are. I have known a few people in my life who had a similar gift for storytelling, the natural gift, the gift of one who is native to life itself, so to speak, and that gift seemed to me to always be a sure sign of a large and generous intelligence. I knew a boy in the army like that, many (how many) years ago. But I don't think I've ever known anyone else besides you who was so able not only to embody this gift but also (this is the crucial thing) to *give* it, so precisely and so naturally. Your letters are always a joy to me.

Once again, this note of mine is late in response to you, and it will also, alas, be shorter than it ought to. It has been a pleasure to teach and work here in Delaware, but now once again I can feel time closing in on me, and there are still many tasks to be performed and many duties to be met. This afternoon my wife Annie and I must get a train over in Wilmington and ride for a long, long time all the way to Charlottesville, Virginia where some of her relatives live. The visit itself ought to be pleasant, especially because we will have a chance to spend some time with a girl named Lisa Kayan. She is actually Annie's goddaughter, but we really treat her as a niece, and sometimes as a daughter outright. She is eighteen years old, a girl with marvelous natural spirit and good humor, and yet she has a strain of sadness in her still. Her father died in the recent war in southeast Asia. Lisa is dear to us. She spent last August with us in Paris.

But the train journey will be long, and I must do some heavy paper work on the way. Then some on our return journey Sunday, which we will have to make by bus.

Next week is Thanksgiving, and we are to visit with Annie's sister in Pennsylvania. Immediately thereafter, we must travel on to New York City, where I am to take care of some important business at Hunter College, where I ordinarily teach. Also in New York, I am going to read my verses one evening at the Guggenheim Museum.

I have about twenty-five new poems (that is, they haven't appeared in a book yet), and I have been toying with the idea of reading them in New York. But I'm really not sure what I'll do.

One thing I want to do soon is to send you copies of some of these, not necessarily for your comment – you have your own precious work to attend to – but, I hope, for your pleasure, and to give you an idea of what has been accumulating in my notebook during the past year. I can see, looking through the work that I have done, that our discussions of the relation between people and landscapes is very much at the heart of it. (When you love a place, really and almost hopelessly love it, I think you love it even for its signs of disaster, just as you come to realize how you love the particular irregularities and even the scars on some person's face. That happened to me once, and I finally wrote about it in an old book of mine called *Saint Judas*.)

We're leaving for Paris on the evening of December 21st, which is not so far away. Partly because of our sometimes intricate journeys, I will be writing to you more or less substantially once in a while, and more often sending you post cards. I hope you don't mind post cards. They are a way of sharing something, some place or other delight, and they can also, when written and sent truly, offer small wavelets, so to speak, to the rhythm of a correspondence. In Milan, a city in Italy which I care about for many reasons, a working city full of factory people, there is a small church that contains on one wall a beautiful Misericordia (it is Mary, holding out the folds of her gown while poor people gather together there). Nobody knows who painted it, and for my part I don't really want to know. The name doesn't matter now. I went out to see it and light a candle when my father died. (I'm not a Roman Catholic. I don't know what I am.) I'll send you a copy of the picture, if I can find one there.

I'm happy to think of the rooster, as he must be happy with his white hens....Oh, yes: I must tell you that when I spoke recently in Philadelphia, Annie and I spent some time with Sam Hamod and his wife. He wanted particularly to be remembered to you.

I hope you are feeling well and happy.

Love,
Jim

✽

Nice, France
January 9, 1979

Dear Leslie,

We arrived in Paris on the morning of December 22nd and right now I am writing you from the city of Nice, on the Mediterranean. Sketching our plans earlier, we had thought of traveling to the town of Husum in Schleswig-Holstein, in northwest Germany. There's a kind of pilgrimage I still want to make there, to the home of a man to whom I am devoted.* But winter has attacked northern Europe pretty wildly. The last I heard Schleswig-Holstein was under 18 feet of snow. We discreetly

*Theodor Storm

departed from Paris in a snowy dawn a few days ago; and now I am sitting in the Hôtel des Orangers. Just to the right of my shoulder, the tip of a mimosa tree waits at the window; and, a little below it, an orange tree, so help me, bearing fruit. For a long time we've wanted to come here and see for ourselves if the legendary winter of the blue coast is true. Yes, it is. The temperature has stayed around 50 degrees; but there's an enormous concentrated dazzle of sunlight that glances off the sea and through the city and on into the hills. Albert Camus was an Algerian, and once, at the end of the war, sick of the ruin of flesh and soul, he went home for a little while. Trying to be healed, wondering how it was that he was still alive, he realized that his childhood had left what he called an eternal summer in his heart. Leslie, you yourself have written with such final force about the powers of light (and the night, too), that I wonder if you, perhaps, feel the same about your childhood and about the southwest in America.... I must tell you that next week we will travel on to the city of Toulouse. We will be there for about two weeks. There should be time for you to write me, if you have time: c/o Post Restante, Toulouse, France. Nothing would give sharper pleasure than to hear from you again. During my last month or so in Delaware, our correspondence fell silent. I ought to have written you a note before we left, but I just failed, that's all. I want to tell you that I did indeed write a long letter to the Guggenheim Foundation about you. The thing to do now is watch and pray.... For some obscure reason, I've felt concerned about you. You told me earlier in our correspondence that you'd had an operation. Then I assumed that all was well; but I've found myself worrying a little. I do hope that you're all right.... There are steep hills and cliffs behind this city, spreckled with white houses, like a pueblo. Please write to me.

Love,
Jim

Tucson, Arizona
January 23, 1979

Dear Jim,

I'm hoping this letter catches you before you move on. I received your heartening letter some days ago, but was working to meet the deadline for the "new" book – the collection of short writings I call *Storyteller*. It is now at the copy service being xeroxed so I can send it out today. Viking Press seems every year to become more and more like a soup factory – they rush me so – showing no understanding at all – their entire focus is upon their new theories of marketing – anyway, I'm sending them most of the collection to keep them quiet for a while.

I've been wondering where to write to you, and thought about sending a letter with enough postage for Europe but to the Delaware address. I felt lonesome for you. So I was very happy to get the letter, though now I'm anxious about you receiving this one. I should have sent a big scribble, "I'm okay, Jim," to this Toulouse address instead of waiting until now to send a longer message.

I don't mean to worry you – that's not what friends are for. The surgery last year was one of those one-time emergency things – like a burst appendix (Is that how you spell it? Or did I spell the word for the rear section of a technical manual where all the unfamiliar terms are defined?). But, on the other hand, I'm not quite the self I used to know. The puzzle is will I ever be anything like the former "me" again? I'm not too particular – I'd like just to be less tense and a little more calm like I once was. I don't expect to *not* change.

I love Camus so much. I read and reread *The Plague*. I enjoy the *Notebooks*, though sometimes he seems so wary of women and love I feel he is too wise about life. He perhaps needed to know the blue coast was there, was possible, in order to go so deeply into that windy chill winter of the Algerian plague city

– somehow I understood that "place" so well. In New Mexico there are a few days each winter that are dark, and a bitterly cold wind blows dust with bits of snow.

I'm going to send an ærogram to Delaware to be forwarded to your final destination *just to be sure* you and I find each other.

Love,
Leslie

꧁

Tucson, Arizona
January 24, 1979

Dear Jim,

In case the letter I sent yesterday doesn't reach Toulouse in time, I'm sending this to Delaware, hoping someone there will kindly forward it. I don't know what arrangements you make for your mail when you go abroad – I don't know what I'd do either, if I were going – I suppose have it all sent in a box to my final destination abroad.

Today it's gray and "cold" here, which means it's 45° and no sun, but for Tucson that's quite grim. I'm burning mesquite I chopped last evening – I like chopping wood. I like chopping wood better than most "household" chores. A sharp axe is so pleasurable to use, especially on this mesquite which is almost as tough as hardwood.

I wanted to enclose two little excerpts from my new book but when I looked at them just now I realized they won't fit in an ærogram, so I will wait and send them to your next address. My great-grandpa was from Ohio, and somewhere in the back of my mind I associate you and him and Ohio, although Grandpa Marmon never went back. Anyway, today I thought I'd send you those little sections which mention Ohio. I'm reading *Two*

Citizens too, and somehow that made me want to send you something I'd written. "Voices Between Waking and Sleep in the Mountains" moves me so much – the love –

A week from today I'm supposed to do a reading in N.Y. and then go to Washington and then back up to N.Y. for two other readings. I have an apartment to use and everything is fairly well set except back here, where my father, who had promised to stay here with Robert, called last night to say that he can't. Robert is 12 and very independent, but I really can't leave him here for nine days even if the neighbors look in on him, etc. So I don't know yet what to do – I had been counting on my dad to help me, but he's got so much of his own to deal with – no job, no money and his wife expecting a baby in late June. I always manage somehow. I had just turned 18 and was a first semester sophomore at the U. of N.M. when Robert was born. I managed to never miss a semester, not even when he was born. My family can usually help me with him, but the problem this time is that Tucson is so far from Laguna.

Mei-Mei Berssenbrugge (who is presently residing in Room 240, Ramada Inn, Carlsbad, New Mexico, where she's poet-in-the-schools for 6 weeks) told me to see John Cage's book *A Year from Monday* because she felt my idea for structuring the collection (*Storyteller*) was similar to Cage's book – and she's right. Anyway, I've been reading Cage's book and it seems he mentions his father's inventions and how his father was thwarted with his little inventions and devices – Cage seems still to suffer for his father's lost dreams. Sometimes I feel that way about my father, and don't know of any way to help him – I just hurt for him.

The rooster is very proud of his two little white hens and he'd lay down his life for them although they are not nearly his equals in beauty or spirit or intelligence. One of them especially loves to crawl *under* parked cars and motorcycles where she then sits for hours. Her feathers are grimy oily gray and she seems to be very comfortable with her slovenly appearance. The other hen is clean, but she is a throw-back to prehistoric days when reptiles were evolving into winged creatures which finally became birds. But he loves them both so much, and they make him very happy—his feathers are more beautiful than they've ever been. All of which goes to show us something, I guess. So if yesterday's letter misses you in Toulouse maybe you will eventually see this one.

I always resented Shakespeare's use of the delayed messenger in *Romeo and Juliet*, maybe because such things are so ordinary and so possible, and so much can be lost for two people that way.

Love,
Leslie

❦

Albi, France
February 1, 1979

Dear Leslie,

I received your beautiful letter in Toulouse all right. Right now we are in the city of Albi. Before I go on, let me tell you that, if you plan to write to me between February 1st and February 14th you should send the letter c/o American Express, Damrak 66, Amsterdam, Holland. Then, if you write between February 15th and February 28th the address is c/o American Express, 11 rue Scribe, Paris, France. I'm sorry, truly, but these are some of the complications of our travels.

I was so happy to hear from you. We must keep faithfully in touch. It's a pleasure and a relief to know that *Storyteller* (I assume it will include the wonderful story of the same title) is now sent to Viking. You sounded rather upset about their manners. In this respect, I feel very lucky in my relations with my publisher, Farrar, Straus and Giroux. My editor there, Michael di Capua, is a lovely guy. We've become good friends over the years, and I can't imagine a more patient, understanding and skilled editor. And he is certainly skilled. I remember vividly his working for hours and hours on end with the novelist Larry Woiwode on his difficult and superb long book called *Beyond the Bedroom Wall.* Do you know that novel, by the way? Woiwode is a fine writer, roughly your age, perhaps a couple of years older.

The city of Albi is in the countryside, situated on the river Tarrn, up the river some kilometres from the large (and noisy and rough) city of Toulouse. Like so many other French towns, Albi is very old. Of course, the modern world has entered the area. There is the main drag along the edge of Albi named for the late Georges Pompidou, who is now dead (and, I trust, urinating battery acid on a live wire in Hell, waiting to be relieved by Nixon), but the old city of Albi is beautifully preserved. It is sort of poised on a bluff high over the river. Set solidly in stone near the edge stands the indescribable huge cathedral of Ste. Cecile, which was originally a fortress; and next to it is the palace where the painter Toulouse Lautrec's mother saved more than 600 of his drawings and paintings. He was a very great genius, and it is exhilarating to be in his presence....I miss badly your letters, and we mustn't lose touch again. I am slowly getting some work done. Please do write to me soon.

Love,
Jim

[The following message was sent on a post card from Holland. The post card was a reproduction of Jan Vermeer's "Young Woman Reading a Letter," from the Rijksmuseum in Amsterdam.]

February 22, 1979

Dear Leslie,

I just received here in Amsterdam the letter you sent to Delaware. Now, our real *home* address is 529 East 85th Street, New York, N.Y. 10028. But I've received your letter in Toulouse okay. I think I wrote you from England...and especially want you to have this card. There are only 36 paintings by Vermeer in existence, and this morning we sat for a long time in a little room with four of them. We were very quiet. There didn't seem to be anything else to say....We'll be here for a week and then back to Paris, where I hope to hear from you. I'll try to write a letter before then.

Love,
Jim

❁

Tucson, Arizona
March 2, 1979

Dear Jim,

The post card of Vermeer arrived yesterday. I have been car rying this ærogram around with me these past days waiting for a time when I could write to you with some semblance of peace. If I am frantic when I write, it sometimes affects the person receiving the letter; I don't want that.

The afternoon I wrote to you about the rooster and his hens we came back to the ranch to find them gone – the little white hens almost without a trace – and piles of rooster's green and bronze and black feathers scattered everywhere. By searching carefully I found four white feathers a short distance from the house. The coyotes had come – at least four of them I think because otherwise the dogs could have protected rooster and his hens. Coyotes waste nothing and so it is as if the white hens were never here; the rooster, on the other hand, was always a strange creature. A number of times I would be talking to Denny and would feel as if we were not alone; when I looked out the open window I'd find the rooster listening outside like a being out of some Haitian voodoo story. Now when the wind blows I find feathers, every time thinking that surely *now* I am seeing them for the last time, but finding them again and again. What is remarkable though are the colors of the feathers, which remain undimmed, and the texture of the feathers, which is as glossy as if they had only just fallen from him; and all this after weeks of the feathers blowing around the ground in dust and rain.

He was a mean and dirty bird but we loved him in a strange sort of way. Our friends who had been pursued or jumped by rooster find it difficult to appreciate our loss. I guess I am still surprised at the feeling we had for him – to realize that without wanting to, without any reason to, he had been dear to us. We are told we should love only the good and the beautiful, and these are defined for us so narrowly. Monday I will be 31. Maybe it has taken me this long to discover that we are liable to love anything – like characters in old Greek stories who set eyes on an oak tree or a bucket and fall in love hopelessly, there are no limits to our love.

Even on the post card I can appreciate the vitality in Vermeer's paintings and how alive they remain by bringing something seldom touched in ourselves alive too – life-giving process, as with the listeners who make it possible for the storyteller to go on. How soothing to be able to sit in that room with the paintings and feel this.

The bay mare will foal in two weeks, and the old sorrel a month later, in April sometime. I hope the bay foals before I leave to teach in Seattle. It has been such a long time since I've seen a new foal. I expect our foals will have a terrible time with the cactus since it seems that no one, no matter how wise or cautious, escapes run-ins with the cholla. There are a number of varieties of cholla, as you probably know. The teddy bear cholla has spines as thick and fuzzy – soft looking – as its name; but the jumping cholla is best-named: careful as you might be as you walk past it, you'll feel it stuck in your sleeve and you can only conclude that it jumped on you. Cholla are good teachers; we all learn their lesson very fast. The colts will too.

After March 23, I will be in Seattle. Mail can be sent to English Department, U. of Washington, Seattle 98195. From April 9th-29th I will be at Vassar College in Poughkeepsie, N.Y. After April 29th I'll be back in Seattle until June 6th or so.

I hope to be able to write to you more frequently once I reach Seattle. Things here in Arizona are lately so unsettled – I suppose because I must leave to teach in Seattle. Anyway, I deeply appreciate your letters and cards – it is as if the letters and cards bring me along with you and Annie in your travels.

Love,
Leslie

❀

Paris, France
March 9, 1979

Dear Leslie,

It's been far too long since I've written you a proper letter and even this one is likely to be unsatisfactory. We have been in (and around) Paris for the past five days, seeing some friends and taking care of several kinds of important business. About two-thirds of it seems to be done at this point. Today is Friday. Very early Sunday morning we will take the long train from Paris all the way to Verona, Italy. I'm not sure, but I think I've already mentioned to you that we will be in Verona from Monday, March 12th, through the following two weeks. Then we will travel on by way of Florence to Rome, and it is really in Rome (c/o American Express) that I will hope to hear from you.

For several reasons too complicated to describe at the moment, we've revised our itinerary. Everything on the previous itinerary (I sent you this, didn't I?) remains the same through our time in Naples, but after we leave Naples the plan for mail is as follows: if you should write to me when we are in Taranto (c/o Poste Restante, Taranto, Italy) you should mail your letter no later than April 14th; next, c/o Poste Restante, Bari, Italy, no later than April 28th; next, c/o Albergo Griffone, Sirmione, Italy, no later than June 10th; finally, c/o La Calcina, Zattere 780, Venice, Italy (mail to be sent no later than July 7th). An important point: when I say mail should be sent no later than a given date, I mean you should post it by that date.

I'm sorry this sounds so confused and confusing. What has happened is that we've decided not to go to Greece at all, but instead to spend an entire month – from May 26th through June 26th – in the truly blessed town of Sirmione. It lies at the end of a green peninsula that sticks way out into the immense blue water of Lake Garda, which is long and skinny and stretches deeper and deeper into the Italian Alps. Well. Then from July 22nd till the end of August and a little beyond, we will be living in Paris, where our address will be c/o Dr. Robert Higgins, 3 rue Ernest Cressons, Paris, France.

But I'd better inform you of a single mailing address just as they come up on the calendar. For example, if you should feel like writing me when you receive this rather sorry present letter, you should send your reply to Verona no later than March 14th.

I've just read over this letter and it looks muddled and silly. But I have missed you very much. I promise faithfully to write again early next week.

Love,
Jim

✿

Verona, Italy
March 14, 1979

Dear Leslie,

The small city of Bruges in Belgium is off by itself, away from Brussels, still some miles from the sea. Centuries ago, Bruges was a seaport. But remember that Belgium is one of the low countries, the Netherlands, and the sea has long since been silted up and over and back, till now there are only long winding canals. We arrived at the station in Bruges on a rainy afternoon a couple of weeks ago. It was strange to walk away from the station toward the town, for a heavy mist involved everything, and only a dim tower or two would reveal part of itself from time to time as the mist parted. We turned a corner at the end of a long street where the old low houses began to recede into the mist, and we came to a small bridge with a huge canal beneath it. It was still winter, but the warmth was beginning to stir things up. On a big slab of ice that was melting about halfway across the canal, a large flock of birds – mallards, moorhens or something that looked like them, and two swans – were in conversation.

The mist rose a little while after we were settled at the hotel in the town square. And so I found Bruges, a revelation. Among the low houses, with the delicacy of their roofs and gables, there are an astonishing number of towers, some of churches, others of municipal buildings. And everywhere there are bells, from the deep-throated bell of the church of St. Salvator to the carillons of the great tower of the city hall. You must imagine what it would sound like, the one hundred and thirty-five small bells of the great carillon all ringing out together, the musicians inside providing intricate patterns like those of a fine organist improvising, and the notes filling the air of the entire town.

As we strolled slowly, as we always do, morning and afternoon and very late evening through the narrow and exquisitely beautiful streets, we found some shops where lace was for sale. Among several places in northern Europe where the weaving of lace is still practiced as an old traditional art, Bruges is one of the finest. Sometimes I wonder about things like lace, things that human beings make with their own hands, things that aren't much help as shelter from the elements or against war and other kinds of brutality. Lace was obviously no help to the Belgians during two horrifying invasions in this century. Nevertheless, the art continues to survive, the craftsmen weaving away with the finest precision over their woofs and spools.

I found some nice examples of this lace and I have one for you. It is enclosed. Happy birthday from Annie and me.

Though most of this letter is about Bruges, we are right now in Verona, Italy, where a couple of days ago I received your beautiful – and very sad – letter. Of course I never saw your rooster, and he never had a chance to jump me, but I can share your feelings for him, and for the small white hens. What you wrote about the improbability of loving this fierce little creature struck me very deep, because your words are so close to a passage in Spinoza's *Ethics*. The passage has given me some pain, but finally it is heartening and bracing, because it is, in my own view, the clearest statement of the plain truth that I know. Spinoza says that the human being is a miraculous creature, and his miracle consists in his capacity for love. He can love anything, from an atom all the way to God. But it is just here, says Spinoza, that the tragic difficulty arises. For man must realize that his capacity for love gives him no right to demand that anyone love him in return. Not anyone. Not even God. I have found that a hard thing to face, but there is something in it that goes beyond pain. Frost wrote, "it must be I want life to go on living."

I'm happy that you'll be in Seattle for a little while. Up there in the English Department you might say hello for me to old friends I made when I studied there: David Wagoner, Jack Leahy, David Fowler, Wayne Burns, William Machett...any number of fine people.

Leslie, we'll be in Verona for a couple of weeks yet, and then we go to Florence for a week (where, if you have time, you might write me c/o Poste Restante). But you sound busy, and Rome will probably be best. Take care of yourself, and have good journeys.

Love,
Jim

Seattle, Washington
April 2, 1979

Dear Jim,

"We won't lose touch," I vow at 1 a.m. reading *Two Citizens*, and now grab hold of this red pen. Your letter with the lace, and the thought of how lace must not be much good in wars, brought me somehow to the blossoming trees, so white I can only think of a snowstorm, and how vulnerable (but of course that's the "good" of the lace – that it is *no good* against bullets –

something like the rooster who was *no* damn good at all, making him precious indeed) the budded trees are in late winter storms. But no winter storms here, and I suppose nobody was ever in Seattle in spring without spending much time looking at the trees. I want to call them by familiar names – pear, apple or peach – but then I hesitate because any place that also has tulip trees and dogwoods might also have others more exotic. It reminds me that we want names for trees unless we can see them together and know which avenue of white blossoming trees I write about. Apple, pear or peach *tells* me *something*, but what of a tulip tree or dogwood – I wonder why the *dog* in dogwood, or the balloon shapes in the tulip tree.

Years ago I read Spinoza and remembered what he said about good deeds (though it was really the same as his statement that you wrote about in your letter). It was that if we *do* something, we do so with no expectations of acknowledgement or reward or even like treatment. We do so only for ourselves, only to know that we have done it in that way. It was so good to think about Spinoza again after all these years – I'll go to the library and find one of the books again.

The students in my classes seem very enthusiastic and ready to do much writing. My mood this spring is more for poems than for fiction, but U. of W. needed fiction classes most, I guess. On April 8th, I'll leave them with a large assignment (after spending these two weeks meeting each one of them individually, outside of class, to get them started) and head for Poughkeepsie for 3 weeks.

I took a short walk along the south shore of Lake Washington yesterday afternoon. It was pretty much deserted except for one sailboat and some ducks near shore. I don't know what kind of ducks they are – some I've never seen before – but their bills are stark white like surgeons' gloves.

Before I left Tucson I found *Moments of the Italian Summer* and *Shall We Gather at the River* at my favorite used book store.

Moments falls open to page 11, "The Language of the Present Moment," and once again I seem to have eyes especially for two lines:

> Limone, wreath of the Garda mountains, the stone villa of
> Catullus still stands down at the far southern end of the lake.
> I hope you are in blossom when his ghost comes home.

It is really that last line I love most, though I could not have loved it so without all the preceding lines, of course. Certain lines remain with me forever. I don't know why.

The trouble is I've never said good-bye to anyone I love. Where most people learn is with death, but at Laguna the dead are not gone, so no need to say good-bye. Aunt Susie is 106 and she talks about getting out of there soon (the nursing home her children, my cousins, have put her in). She'll get around to writing out the stories then, she says, in far greater detail than she's ever been able to tell them – over at Cliff House, she says, with Tsa'na'di, her mother's sister, an aunt who was only a few years older than she. "She's living over there, now," Aunt Susie tells me, and at first I think she means the old family house near Pugate Village when she says Cliff House, because the familiarity in her tone as she talks assures me that it is close and well-known to all of us. But then I remember Tsa'na'di died twenty years ago. Still, Jim, I know by her matter-of-fact tone and the warmth in her voice she is *not* talking about dying; Cliff House is no romantic metaphor; it's the place she is going when she gets out of there.

Love,
Leslie

P.S. Thank you so *much* for the lace.

Taranto, Italy
April 27, 1979

Dear Leslie,

According to the schedule you sent to me a while ago, you should be in Poughkeepsie right now, getting ready to return to Seattle in two more days. I hope this letter will be waiting for you there.

I hope you will write to me in Sirmione, though we won't be there for a couple of weeks yet. At the moment we are in the seaport town of Taranto, a lovely and kind of sad city set in the instep of the Italian boot. I am sitting right at a balcony looking out over an inland water called the Piccolo Mare, the little sea. It is still early evening. The fishing boats, even the small ones, are coming in, and the men are gathering in their small nets that you can see them sometimes mending in the sunlight in the old city across the bridge. Men go fishing with their children here, and it is hard work. It is common to see a father working with his small son, whether fishing or sewing nets. There is something deeply consoling about the sight of such things, which have been going on for literally thousands of years. One doesn't have to turn one's face away from the wars, the terrible things. Tarento is one of those strategically important places that have been raked over and bombed over and massacred over by everyone from the barbarians to the Saracens to the Turks to the Germans to the Americans to God knows who else. But other things, other things fully as true: Lysippis and Praxiteles worked here long ago, and the latter left an incredibly beautiful girl's face. Pythagoras, our old high school chum, came here and walked in the groves, pondering the right triangles in mid-air. And, believe it or not, Plato came here for visits. Now we are all graying and dark and Italian, and this evening later I will celebrate one brief pause in the annals of warfare by eating the local pasta, *orchiette* (little ears), and easing my heart(burn) with mineral water.

Although it hasn't been so terribly long, it seems very long since I've heard from you. I hope you are well and happy, and that your visits to Washington and Poughkeepsie have been good. We saw Frank MacShane and his family in Rome, and we talked of you with the warmest admiration.

Love,
Jim

❦

Seattle, Washington
May 10, 1979

Dear Jim,

I took a supply of these ærograms with me when I went to Poughkeepsie for those three weeks, but I left behind your updated itinerary, taking instead another letter you'd send me. Anyway, here I am finally. The resident writer position at Vassar kept me busier than I imagined it would – I spent a good deal of time working individually with the students. Fiction is so time-consuming to deal with. Here at Seattle I've been frantically trying to read and comment upon the work the fiction students did here while I was gone. Instead of 30 students, I ended up with 51, and so it's made things difficult. Also, despite previous arrangements, the U. of Washington campus newspaper is attempting to make a "cause" out of the fact that I was away from the campus for 3 weeks – I discover that it is a part of a longer conflict at this campus over students getting their money's worth from courses. Of course fiction writing is hardly like a chemistry class, but people who go looking for causes seldom think much about such details. I am trying to calm myself and let the English Department handle these goings-on, since all this was okayed by the Department, but it still upsets me. I have put in more time with these students, especially individually or in small groups, than I have ever given students anywhere.

I talk with my students about narrative writing instead of separating poetry from fiction exactly.... I read to them from your *Moments of the Italian Summer.*

The mares have foaled now – the first is a bay filly we've named La Araña, for the spidery legs she has. Her mother was a race horse briefly – in the starting gate of her first race she reared with her jockey and fell backwards, injuring the rider and ending her career. Since we've had the mare, we've learned she has a few "quirks" about being enclosed and have discovered that otherwise she is a fine mare. I hope to spend a great deal of time with La Araña so that she will not be as touchy as her mother is about enclosures. The second foal is from our big sorrel mare, who is 18 years old and a "classic" American quarter horse – i.e., capable of carrying a 189-pound rider and 40-pound saddle for 12 hours at a stretch over rough terrain. She is a sorrel like her dam, and we will call her La Rojeña because her mother's name is Mamba Roja.

My mother's mother lives in Portland. Grandma Jessie is 87, and my cousin who lives in Seattle and I brought her up last week for a visit. Grandma looks more and acts more like 67 than 87 even though she broke her hip last November. While she was here she got to talking and she mentioned her rooster. I told her I never knew she had a rooster, and she said yes, old Mr. So-and-so had given her a baby rooster and hen because his neighbors complained about the rooster crowing at 2 a.m. Grandma Jessie kept him tied to a big chestnut tree in her backyard but sometimes he slipped the cord off his foot and flew over the fence. "Old Grandpa Leslie stepped off the porch where the hen was eating scraps and stepped on her head and killed her" (that was my grandma's father-in-law who lived with them for a time). I asked her whatever became of the rooster, and she said that *her* neighbors finally complained about his crowing and she had to give him to friends who lived farther outside Portland. I only mention this because my Grandma Jessie seems so much a city woman, even now with her pinochle and bridge-playing and her happiness in a city apartment. It seems so unlikely that she would even have had a rooster, but she did at one time.

I am anxious to get back to my own writing, but realize that for a few weeks I must concentrate on my students. I have a number of students who are writing very fine pieces and I am happy to be working with them, regardless. It's only sometimes I get lonesome for my own work.

I sent you a copy of Mei-Mei Berssenbrugge's new book which she gave me to pass on to you. I am too close to the work in the book to be very reliable, but I love what she has done. Part two of "Rabbit, Hair, Leaf" is from a time she spent at the little stone house by the sandstone cliffs south of Acoma. The place appears in my novel—where the springs flow out of the cliffside. Part two of "Commentary" she wrote after helping me with my long narrative of the storyteller's escape. The shawl Mei-Mei mentions is the shawl the heat made around my old storyteller, though of course all of this has nothing really to do with what Mei-Mei has written or that I have written. Still, I like to see the relationships—just as I see what writing to you, Jim, about roosters, has helped me to discover another dimension of storytelling in my family. For this and for your dear and beautiful letters I want to thank you.

I am feeling a little lonely tonight and wishing this might be conversation and not a letter, though I love the letters just as much – you understand, I think. I miss you – take good care of yourself and Annie.

Love,
Leslie

Fano, Italy
May 23, 1979

Dear Leslie,

According to the schedule you sent me, you will be in Seattle "till June 6 or so." I'm hoping this letter will reach you there. If it doesn't I trust your mail will be forwarded.

I think I last wrote to you from Taranto, on the instep arch, way down on the Ionian Sea. We wandered, exploring a good deal all over Apulia, and when finally we came to the big port of Bari, and spent ten days there, we were exhausted, in spirit if not in body. Bari itself, at least in its new section where we had to stay, is an ugly town, overcrowded with vicious and frightening people. I don't want to disillusion you about Italy. I love this country very much. In Europe, at least, it is incomparably beautiful, and people almost everywhere are warm and humane. But you must be aware of the strange form that political and social unrest is taking in Italy these days. The so-called Red Brigades have intensified their destructive actions during recent weeks, because the general elections are to take place June 3rd, and the terrorists have openly announced their intention to destroy them. One evening while we were visiting the exquisitely lovely, golden, sun-blanched city of Lecce, the Communists held a rally devoted to a repudiation of the terrorists; for on that very day the Red Brigades had bombed the chief offices of the Christian Democrats in Rome, killed some people and injured many others. So the Communists, of all things, were coming to the support of their political opponents. Both the extreme leftists and the moderates in Italy are beleaguered by these terrorists, and everybody in Italy is wondering just who they are. In my opinion, they are an extension of what we found in Bari. The streets day and night are menacingly full of swaggering, sneering young bullies of both sexes. They are teenagers. Now the record companies and the television commercials have created an image of the righteous and glorified adolescent. But I am old enough to remember that the word "youth" has a sinister history in this God-forsaken century. "In the highest sense the young are always right," said Baldur Von Sirach, head of the Hitler Jugend. It was the political genius of the Nazis to know how to use punks like those we saw in Bari.

Please excuse this depressing letter.

Love,
Jim

❦

Sirmione, Italy
May 28, 1979

Dear Leslie,

I'm sending this letter to your address in Tucson, because you said you'd be in Seattle only till June 6th or so. I'm allowing about ten days between here and the U.S.A. (that may be too much or too little, depending on the caprice of the Italian mails). Anyway, this ought to reach you in Tucson all right.

I'm happy that you enjoy the lace handkerchief from Belgium. The craftsmen there have done some truly spectacular things. And thank you so much for sending Mei-Mei's new book. I had seen some of the poems before. I like the entire book very much, and I wish you would send me her address so that I can write to her about it. We've met her a couple of times, most interestingly at the Kinnells' house in New York City. She is a remarkable person, and a fine poet.

It's interesting that you should have found *Moments of the Italian Summer* in Tucson. Much of that little book was written right here where I am sitting and writing to you now. Yesterday or so I sent you a post card with a photograph by air of Sirmione. Beautiful Catullus, who used to come here and visit friends during the summer so many centuries ago, called it almost an island, and, in a curious old phrase, "the eye of all islands." I've always thought this must have been a healing place for him. His poems about people in Rome are brillant beyond measure, but they are truly violent, full of hair-raising torture of feeling. He must have been an odd kind of guy. But my God, he could sing like a bird.

Your paragraph about your Aunt Susie is very beautiful. That sense of the dead's presence is – well, it makes me think of something I've wanted to ask you. Have you ever read Willa Cather's novel *The Professor's House*? Its middle section is a narration by a young man named Tom Outland who had discovered a Pueblo city way up in a cliff in the southwest. I think it is one of the best things I have ever read about America.

What has happened to your new book? And, though I hesitate to ask, what about your Guggenheim application?

Please write to me here. We won't leave till June 25th.

Love,
Jim

[The following message was sent on a post card from Sirmione, Italy. The photograph on the card was an ærial view of Lake Garda.]

May 26, 1979

Dear Leslie,

In the foreground of this photo is the town of Columbare, and Sirmione, where we are now, is way out in the background, surrounded by the lake, the very breast of the grand land. I'm happy that you like the lace handkerchief from Belgium. The last letter I sent you was kind of depressed, but really Italy is very beautiful, and I feel happy now. Sirmione is a divine place. Please write to us here c/o Albergo Griffone.

Love,
Jim

❦

Sirmione, Italy
June 4, 1979

Dear Leslie,

Of course I can't know whether or not the world looks strange to God. But sometimes it looks strange to me. In the same mail with your letter of May 10th, which I received about three days ago, I heard from Lois Shelton, director of that Poetry Center at the University of Arizona in Tucson. She'd earlier invited me to speak there in the fall of 1979, but I never received the letter. So now she's asked me to come down in the spring of 1980. Annie and I will certainly come there. We don't know yet the exact date, but it will be in spring.

And right at the end of your May 10th letter, you spoke of wanting to have a conversation sometimes in addition to letters.

Having mentioned this matter, I suddenly realize, kind of apprehensively, that you might well not be in Tucson next spring. Well, never mind. For all I know, you might well be there, too. In any case, we will certainly meet and have good long walks and talks some time or other. But I was very moved that those two letters arrived at the same time. The world can go on being as strange as it likes, for all of me. There are good signs appearing in it from time to time.

I am distressed for you to hear about the editorializing of the students at the University of Washington about your visiting Vassar during the semester. But I am not surprised. I have been a full-time professor for some twenty years. The students who gouge their way into the staffs of campus newspapers are almost always superficially clever adolescents who, for those few college years, have managed to get themselves into a position from which they can fulfill their dreams of power: having print at their disposal, they have the easy opportunity to be snotty and even to inflict wounds without having to face the consequences of the wounds. Wounds bleed. But the students don't think it's blood. They still think it's ketchup. What I have learned to do is exactly what you have done: to make sure that the authoritative people in the department know exactly what I am doing and where I am going, and when, and why. Hell doesn't break loose much these days, simply because I seldom speak in public. But at the least sign of hell, I send the complainers to the English Department.

Please write me c/o La Calcina, Zattere 780, Venice.

Love,
Jim

❀

Sirmione, Italy
June 15, 1979

Dear Leslie,

We are still in Sirmione. We leave for Venice in ten days.

Not a morning has passed here without my working steadily, and I hope steadfastly, at this table for several hours. I have been trying to make sense out of this year's European notebook, which has gone way past three hundred pages. I am somewhat taken aback to realize that I have made more or less workable versions of exactly thirty new pieces. At least, I have revised them and copied them into a larger notebook. Now they will have to lie there by themselves for a while until they change. They almost always do. A poem is a very odd duck. It goes through changes – in form and color – when you leave it alone patiently, just as surely as a plant does, or an animal, or any other creature. Have you ever read a book by someone which you *know* has been written too quickly and impatiently and then published too soon? Such books always remind me of tomatoes or oranges that have been picked still green and then squirted full of artificial colors. They look nice on the supermarket shelves, and they taste awful. I remember reading such books and feeling the glands under my chin begin to ache. They made me feel as though I were getting the mumps.

Well, this new work of mine will change in time. Some of it is naturally ripening already. Before long I will send you three new little prose pieces, and see what you think.

The weather here on Lake Garda has been behaving strangely. Early in the morning the mountains around the lake reveal themselves with dreadfully powerful clarity in the air, but then, as often as not, a heat haze obscures them by the afternoon. But last evening – I swear it was nine o'clock and after – we saw a storm, a rain storm, crawl up over and down the side of

Monte Baldo, totally cover the town of Bardolino across the lake, and then, right in the midst of the gray rain, reveal a rainbow. A brilliant one, in the rain, right after the sun had long gone down. It is a strange place.

Please write, dear friend. I hope you are well.

Love,
Jim

❁

Tucson, Arizona
June 16, 1979

Dear Jim,

I wonder if it is the size of these ærograms that inhibits me, or if it is the uncertainty of my life right now – anyway I know my letters haven't been much good except to let you know that I look forward to yours and they reassure me with your calm and with your good eyes for the whereabouts of Catullus' ghost.

I have just returned from a short visit at Laguna – I went over for the child custody case and lost; I'm hoping my former husband will be generous with allowing visits, and I have Caz with me, and Robert, for 5 weeks this summer. I did not get to spend more than two days at Laguna this time but I thought a great deal about two of my father's first cousins, Jack and Les, both dead now – Les died while I was here in Tucson. He wasn't old, but he was one of the men I was writing about when I wrote *Ceremony*. Les had been a football star at the U. of New Mexico for one semester before he was drafted. The local press called him "Squaw" because he was Laguna. He was over six feet tall and even these last years he was a strong man – except I guess for what the liquor did. I suppose it might be because a good part of him became part of the main characters of the novel that I spent some time yesterday looking at the house he and his brother Jack had lived in. It was the house my father was born in – an old house passed around in the family until Jack and Les, and now it has reverted back to the village, i.e., the Laguna community. I grew up in that house and the roof was bad when I was ten; yesterday I could see how the big sheets of corrugated tin were flapping in the wind and not much longer was the old house going to stand. But it takes more than one generation for old buildings or old drunks to be forgotten at Laguna – all because of the stories, I guess. It is in this way people at Laguna still refer to the store at the corner as "Joe's." They always say they are walking down to Joe's store, but it's been eleven years since Joe accidentally or purposely fired the .38 into his chest. In two or three generations it will be known as someone else's store – but for how long, I suppose, depends on how much that person gives the rest of Laguna to talk about. This was my second divorce, while Laguna is just now learning about divorce at all. I'm the only Leslie left now, except for Les's presence as I've already outlined it to you. I suppose Les will be remembered for being called "Squaw" in the *Albuquerque Journal* and for his car wrecks and brawls; and it's shaping up that I am known now for my husbands; many of the older people who remembered me for the horses I was always training and riding and falling off – so many of them are gone now. I would rather be remembered for the horses.

I think I will be here in the spring of 1980 and can hardly wait to talk with you and to meet Annie. I never know anything for certain but I hope to resign from the University of New Mexico soon, although I will teach a last course over there this fall.

The new book will have old photographs from Laguna, mostly taken by my grandfather and my father. Thus is still isn't "in the works" quite yet – my editor likes to transmit the whole thing together so things aren't quite lost: a good idea with the photographs.

I'm glad you like Mei-Mei's new book. Her address is Box 685, El Rito, New Mexico. I'll send this as #1 and also a #2 letter.

Love,
Leslie

❀

Tucson, Arizona
June 27, 1979
#2 letter

Dear Jim,

As you can see from the date on letter #1, I *do* intend to write – and you, dear friend, are the only person I am able to correspond with these days. I feel particularly mute with members of my own family and other friends who know too well the recent events – the court custody fight, etc. There's not really anything to say about it, but I feel a tension – people expecting an explanation or accounting. I suppose I might just be imagining this, but anyhow, I can't write to anyone.

How wonderful to hear that you've got so much written! That is so reassuring – to know that when the new pieces are "ripe" we will receive a wonderful new book from you. There are gifts which come but are not accountable in the usual ways – I know this when I remember your lines about Catullus' ghost and Lake Garda – they come back to me suddenly and predictably (I might be feeding the mares) but the feeling which comes is so peaceful and healing. I think to myself then, Jim, that however many times I thank you for the writing you've given us, there will never be thanks enough.

My mainstay now is the writing, though all I can do is dream of the stories I want to work with. I fret over the chaos which prevents me from working at my full capacity, but perhaps these passages of time can function as gestations too, as you indicate your new pieces must also be left alone to grow themselves. I write a few little notes to accompany the old photographs which I've convinced Viking to allow me to include with the writing. The photographs were taken by my father and my grandfather and go back to the 1890s in the Laguna Pueblo area. After I began considering using the photographs I realized that all I've ever known about my great-grandpa Marmon is the stories I've heard and the old photographs we have of him; and yet *I feel* as if I was alive when he was, though of course I was not. At least part of this sense of him, I see now, comes from these old photographs. Still, I'm wary of the unexpected (or maybe "unpredictable" is a better term) effect that the juxtaposition of these photographs with the writing may produce. I've always been curious about narrative being combined with visual images. I hope to have the entire manuscript with all the photographs delivered to Viking by July 15th. On July 21st, the producer, director, drama director and I will be meeting at Laguna to begin pre-production planning for the pilot film in my Laguna film project. The proposal for money to make the pilot film must be in Washington, D.C., by the end of November. The Laguna people working with me are very excited about the production and filming, and once again *I am excited* about the film making. Film is so tedious and expensive – I'm so thankful to work with words on paper, depending on no one. With film there are so many collaborators one must have – but I will try it just this one time.

Please forgive my delinquent letter-writing – I shall be more attentive, Jim, I promise.

Love,
Leslie

Venice, Italy
July 18, 1979

My dear Leslie,

Just returned from Tuscany and Umbria to Venice and preparing to go on to Paris where we will spend the month of August before returning to America. I found the two letters from you.

I want to talk to you about something. In 1962, my first wife and I were divorced in Minneapolis. She moved to California, where she has remarried and worked as a nurse ever since. My older boy, Franz, was about 8 at the time. He and I maintained correspondence. He worked desperately hard at school, and distinguished himself in high school. He went on to graduate from Oberlin in Ohio, where he is living at the moment. He has become a writer, and he has talent. But strange, distressing things began to happen to my younger son, Marshall. He was always in devilment at school, and never finished high school, although he took one of those ridiculous California tests that provide the "equivalent" of a high school diploma. Over the years I've heard from him occasionally, and he visited me several times, particularly after Annie and I were married 12 years ago. Marshall spent a summer with us in Montreal, some time in New York, some time in Paris and in Hawaii. But in Hawaii he had undergone (already) what amounted to an abrupt change of personality, and his mother told me that he had had bad experiences with drugs. So things went on, and I didn't hear from him directly.

But last fall he phoned me suddenly in a long and terrifying speech barely coherent, full of anger and confusion. Shortly afterward I received a letter from him. He told me that he did not want me as his father.

Since that time, I have kept in touch with his mother, and I'm helping financially without his knowledge. Annie has been a great support through it all, but I have mainly clung to my books, my writing....Leslie, I am not telling you all this in despair, and I ask you to forgive me for laying out my worst pain to you. I just wanted somehow to tell you that I understand how you feel about your children.

Love,
Jim

✾

Tucson, Arizona
July 5, 1979

Dear Jim,

U. of Washington forwarded my mail this week and I found the postcard you sent from Lake Garda and the letter from Fano. Well, tonight I am thinking about the Lake Garda of your "Language of the Present Moment" and wondering about the use of the old photographs in my new book. I realized tonight how incomparable is the beauty of your words, and how inarticulate photographs, can be. I wonder if it is a wise decision to include the old photographs with the little stories – will the snapshots my grandfather took in 1930 undercut the view I give with the stories? I *do* know that one must *not* follow a description of a house with a photograph of the same, but it occurs to me now that just seeing how Laguna looks may affect the reader's sense of the little stories.

I have discovered, though, since I began looking through my grandma's collections of old photographs, that much of what I "remember" of places and people is actually a memory of the photograph of the place and person, but that I had forgotten the photograph and remembered it as if I had been told about it. There were always many stories that accompanied the evenings we spent with the tall Hopi basket full of photographs.

We would ask Grandpa or Grandma to identify people we did not recognize, and usually we would get a story of some sort along with the person's name. I suppose that may be why I have remembered these old photographs *not* as visual images but as the words that accompanied them; in one sense, of course, the old snapshots are boring or meaningless if one doesn't have an identity of sorts for the person or places in them.

I suppose that is the nature of the snapshot – it needs words with it. Photographs which speak for themselves are art. I am interested now in the memory and imagination of mine which come out of these photographs – maybe I am more affected by what I see than I had heretofore realized. Strange to think that you *heard* something – that you heard someone describe a place or a scene when in fact you saw a picture of it, saw it with your own eyes.

Now that I look at all this it seems so obvious – this is what makes a poet a poet and not a painter or photographer. But *you* have thought this over, Jim, because in *Moments* you have Joan Root's drawings and they have a very subtle but critical effect upon the way I perceive the book. It is as if the drawings create a special quality of silence – not white silence of the blank page (which much poetry and fiction demand) but a murmur of late afternoon sun, a yellow glow of voices in the distance so the voice of the pieces, while clear and distinct, is not alone. The drawings become a sort of chorus (I'm thinking of the classical "chorus" now; my poor wandering senses are with Medea in Greece, not Italy). Well, tomorrow I will have the photographs arranged next to the pages of manuscript and I suppose I will discover whether I have a chorus or simply confusion....

It has been hot with only enough rain to make the air heavy; but this weather brings out exotic varieties of lizards which are larger than my hand and iridescent colors – blues and greens.

They pose on shady walls and window screens unconcerned with human beings; they seem not to be feeding at these times, but simply reposing. I think it has been too hot for snakes except at night; even after sundown the ground will burn your belly if that is how you travel. The lizards, I notice, run on their toe tips, their bellies and chests carried well off the ground. The saguaro fruit is ripening and I think the scarlet pulp is much more exciting than the white blossoms – though certainly they are lovely – but the fruit pods are visible for half a mile against the green. Birds we never see otherwise have begun to arrive for the feasting – it only lasts two weeks, and then they will be gone again. At one time small Sonoran parrots might have come from the south, but now you only see them in a cage at the Desert Museum. Still, I'm always watching for bright green and yellow feathers because they might show up some year.

When you and Annie come next spring I hope we can take a short walk up in these hills and I will show you the little I have learned to recognize here. It is a lovely *green* desert – so much green in a hot, dry place – I wonder at it sometimes. I am so excited about your many new poems and send wishes for continuing to you.

Love,
Leslie

❦

Paris, France
July 29, 1979

Dear Leslie,

Your extraordinarily beautiful letter was waiting when we arrived in Paris on July 22nd, just a week ago today. I haven't been able to attempt a proper answer till now. We arrived to learn that we were five days early. Dr. Higgins had sent us a message in Venice which we never received. However, all has gone well anyway. We quickly changed plans and took a train to Moret-sur-Loing.

It is a small medieval village just south of Paris. The Loing is a little river that runs along limpidly and gently past Moret for some miles down to the town of St. Mammes, where in a sudden strange confluence it joins both the Seine and the Marne at once. The very great and enduring impressionist painter Alfred Sisley lived and worked in Moret for twenty-two years, and the citizens of the town and countryside love their earthly place so much that they have kept it thrillingly alive in its old form. We spent a whole day walking along the canal and the river Loing all the way from Moret to St. Mammes and beyond. Sisley painted the light and color here with such precise love that we could feel his angelic luminous spirit everywhere.

Tell me, Leslie: do you know Sisley and his work? Your writings have such a startling power of light and clarity that you remind me of him. That is, one side of your work reminds me of him. You also have something that he does express so strongly: a sense of darkness and human entanglement.

Though I haven't seen your photographs, I am convinced that you have done precisely the right thing in including them with the stories. What you've done is to create, into a single form, a new thing that grows naturally out of two other forms of experience and expression. You say in your letter, "there were always many stories that accompanied the evenings we spent with the tall Hopi basket full of photographs." Surely this is the heart of the book you've described to me, the imaginative heart of it.

In your final paragraph – about the lizards, the birds and the cactus fruit – I do declare, Leslie, something happens to you when you write with your characteristic warmth: you can sing like a bird. Whatever has happened to disrupt your life and feelings, you sound whole and beautiful.

Love,
Jim

❋

Tucson, Arizona
July 28, 1979

Dear Jim,

I am deeply moved by the letter you sent and want you to know that I will always cherish and guard its story. I believe more than ever that it is in sharing the stories of our grief that we somehow can make sense out—no, not make sense out of these things....But through stories from each other we can feel that we are not alone, that we are not the first and the last to confront losses such as these. At Laguna whenever something happens (happy or sad or strange), that vast body of remembered stories is brought forth by people who have been listening to the account of this recent incident. Immediately the listeners, in turn, begin telling stories about the other times and other people from the area who have enjoyed or suffered the same luck, and by the time people get done telling you about all the others who have lost wagons and *whole* teams of horses in the quicksand, you aren't feeling nearly so bad about spending an entire Saturday digging your bay mares out of quicksand. "The word gets around," as they say, and so it all becomes a matter of community knowledge and concern. If something very sad and difficult comes to you, you know that it will take its place with the other stories and that somehow, as a story, it will, from that time on, be remembered and told to others who have suffered losses.

Isolation is so overwhelming at these times—I could feel

myself lying deeper and deeper in it until I could not talk, literally, until I did not want to talk to anyone – my mother, my sisters – about anything. I still only write letters to you, and occasionally to Mei-Mei. I realize now how the telling at Laguna was meant to prevent the withdrawal and isolation at times like this. "The knife cuts both ways" – a corruption, I think, of the homily about double-edged swords and things working both ways. Anyway, people at home also keep account of the funny, the silly, the crazy things that you do too, and the only consolation you have when an embarrassing, funny story about you "gets around" is that *you know* at least one funny, embarrassing story about everyone else or just about everyone else in the village too, and everyone knows that you do, so they won't lay it on you too heavily, not unless they are sort of enemies, and then they know you will resurrect stories about them and on it will go.

What it all means is that it is imperative to keep up with the latest stories, and it is imperative as well to listen to Grandma in case she recalls a very old story about someone or another, because in this scheme of things every story that is remembered has at least some reassurances for you. It is a powerful force and one which must be watched carefully to make sure that persons don't use it destructively. The root of each Navajo healing ceremony is a particular story – by now very *ancient* stories – but the idea is clear: certain stories at certain times have a healing property, especially with your family and friends gathered around as they must be for a Navajo "sing."

I think that in these times especially, but probably for all times, in the stories we tell or share we can only be guided by the heart – we cannot dictate or predict which stories will be "the ones." All we can do is to remember and to tell with all our hearts, not hold anything back, because anything held back or not told cannot continue on with others.

In the new book I have included some very old stories which

I wrote from memory, the way I heard them a long time ago. Memory is tricky – memory for certain facts or details is probably more imaginative than anything, but the important thing is to keep *the feeling* the story has. I never forget that: the *feeling* one has of the story is what you must strive to bring forth faithfully.

In the new book, I have Aunt Susie's story about the little girl who ran away. The years and years (hundreds of years) of telling have stripped it of specific names, and more importantly, of explanations and "reasons" why these things happened. (Sometimes I think "soap opera" originates out of the reasonings, the explanations, the logic that is *imposed* on stories.) The little girl asks her mother to make her some *yastoah* – cornmeal mush boiled until a curled-up crust forms on top of it. Anyway, the mother says that if the girl will go bring firewood, she will make her *yastoah*. The little girl goes down the mesa trail to the flats below and gathers firewood, just where her mother told her to find it. The wood is crooked pieces of juniper branches which the little girl carries back up to her mother. But when the little girl gets it back to the house, the crooked pieces of juniper have become snakes, and her mother tells her she must return the snakes to where she picked them up. The mother does not scold the little girl, she just tells her to take the snakes back. But somehow the little girl's feelings are hurt – maybe because her mother told her to pick up the crooked pieces of wood which turned out to be snakes – I don't know. But the little girl takes off from Acoma, her home, and she heads north. She's going to the lake near Laguna, to drown herself. As she goes, she meets an old man from her home village – he's been out gathering wood, and he sees her hurrying away from home, so he asks her where she's going. She tells him she's going to Ka'waik, the Beautiful Lake, to drown herself because her mother wouldn't make her any *yastoah*. The old man says, "Oh, my dear child! Let me take you back home."

But she runs away from him and he is too old to catch her, so the old man hurries to Acoma to tell the little girl's mother. The mother hurries about and cooks the *yastoah* and she gathers all the little girl's nicest clothing – pretty manta dress, her little flowered shawl, the buckskin moccasins – and the mother hurries after her. The little girl's mother can see her daughter running 'way ahead of her, and the mother calls out to her, but the little girl won't stop – the mother tells her she has her *yastoah* but the little girl won't stop. She is very near the lake now and what she cries is a song:

> My mother, my mother – she wouldn't make me any *yastoah*
> So I'm going to Ka'waik, the Beautiful Lake, and jump in.

At the edge of the lake she pauses to lay a little downy feather in her hair on top of her head – this is done by some clans for the dead – and then the little girl jumps in. The little girl's mother runs to the edge, but all she can see in the water far below is that little feather whirling around and around. The mother is very sad, and when she returns to Acoma mesa, she stands on the cliff and throws the *yastoah* and the little girl's clothing over the edge – she throws them off, but as they fall they become the most beautiful butterflies of all colors – blue ones, yellow ones, red ones and white ones. And so they say that's why you still find such beautiful butterflies around the Acoma area.

I heard this story years ago, but didn't write it down until this past winter. Even then I didn't know why I was remembering it after all that time. But today, Jim, thinking about your letter and what you said suddenly makes it very clear. For this I thank you with all my heart, Jim.

Love,
Leslie

P.S. I saw a little owl the other night and was reminded of your saguaro poem and the little elf owl's face. My youngest son,

Caz, and I were playing rummy at my neighbor's house where we'd gone to water plants for him. It was after dark and the owl must have been attracted by the kitchen light. He perched on the scratching post Tom kept for his cat on the porch deck. (The coyotes got the cat, so the scratching post *had been* rather silly out there, but the owl gave the post a new place in the scheme of things.) This owl was fearless and watched a whole hand of rummy and didn't care if we stared at him or not – he watched us with his big eyes like deep water.

❦

Paris, France
August 8, 1979

Dear Leslie,

It must have been at least four days ago that I received your second letter written on July 28th. It contained what I take to be the second half of your story about the runaway child, the downy feather in her hair as she vanishes in the water, and the mother tossing the things over the cliff and seeing them turn into butterflies. Evidently you were writing in response to what I'd written you about my estranged son.

I had some misgivings about having written you such a letter. You'd just told me about losing the child custody case, and I responded in a rush of impulse. You aren't a person given to expanding at length on your own pain, but the pain was there, and I simply wanted somehow to tell you that I recognize it and, in my own way, share it. But later it occurred to me that my own experience is not typical. To this day I don't understand really why my son turned away from me, and I've never replied to his confused, harsh letter. Perhaps there will be a reconciliation between us sometime. I pray so. Meanwhile, it delighted me very much to think of you and your little boy Caz playing rummy in the evening under the concerned eyes of the small owl. I feared I might be imposing on your private feelings by offering a glimpse of one of my own scars. But no one could live with such passionate imagination, and write as beautifully as you write, without bearing some scars also, and it was these that I wanted to tell you I recognize and – in my own way – bless. We all seem doomed to a freedom to choose between indifference and sadness. I can't – or won't – be indifferent to life, and yet when I turn my face toward it, how sorrowful it seems. Referring obliquely to the beautiful works of art that perished when the Romans destroyed ancient Carthage, Virgil wrote, *sunt lacrimæ rerum* – "These are the tears of things." The phrase has stayed in my mind since I was a boy, likely a troubled boy, long ago, in Ohio.

But I don't want us to drown in the undercurrent of sadness, and I value the presence of that owl sitting with you and watching you play cards. This year I've written a good deal about the non-human presences that, in some message of the spirit, come and sit with us and keep us alive.

Love,
Jim

❦

Tucson, Arizona
August 21, 1979

Sometimes I have so many things to tell you, they won't fit in one of these things – so this is the first part of the letter, Jim.

Dear Jim,

My life has changed a great deal in the past two years, and the changing and moving have left me more alone than I have ever been before – though for one *not* from Laguna, my "aloneness" might seem like a carnival. Anyway, of all the times you might have written to me and this exchange between us have begun, this is the time when I most needed to hear from you. I don't believe in random occurrences or blind chance, though I know the patterns of this world are capricious and terribly complex. I am just thankful that we are so fortunate to find each other again.

The story went to you with the same feelings – grief and love and compassion – that your letter brought to me. In that way we help each other – I never thought about it – it just felt like something I must write to you. I am overwhelmed sometimes and feel a great deal of wonder at words, just simple words and how deeply we can touch each other with them, though I know that most of the time language is the most abused of all human abilities or traits. But as you said, you can't or won't be indifferent. I *realize* many wonderful things about language – "realize" in the sense of feeling or understanding intuitively: I realize such things most often when I am greatly concerned with another person's feelings. I think such realization is one gift which human beings may give each other. I'm not much good at analysis or scholarly efforts with language, probably because I don't value them as much as I value understanding, which is informed by that which is deeply felt before it is examined. So I am happiest that you and I have these letters to each other. With you to write to, I go through the day with a certain attention I might not always have. I look for things you might want to *see* for yourself, but I can't seem to get them into a letter.

Sometimes I even stew about the quality of light here at sundown and the appearances of the clouds. Surely there is some language, probably even English, that can account for the colors which result from this light. But I can only think of the painters who use black velvet instead of canvas because black velvet would seem to be just the medium, when of course it is not. The only way description can begin to match the clouds after sunset is by including the little fossilized clam shells I found on a ridge past Paguate. The stone inside the little shells is a grayish blue with a translucent quality, as though a tiny sun were buried deep somewhere within the shell, though the clouds I am attempting to describe were in the eastern sky after the sun had set and surely they had no sun behind their thick layers and rolls. I finally find that clouds are best compared to belly fat and membrane as they emerge when you are skinning or cleaning a deer. They are such beautiful animals even as you dress them out. But fat like that and even the deer itself came only in years when there had been good rains and plenty of snow...we are back to clouds again. The day I think a scorpion stung me, that day as I was walking up the hill with my sting, I saw among all the clouds that were blood red at sunset one cloud that was somehow shielded or blocked by other clouds so that it alone surrounded by all the others was white or silver-white, as only a cloud at this time of day could be. I stopped to look at it and to try to figure out how to describe it so that its full effect might be conveyed – but felt only the irritation with the limitations I find in myself sometimes, with my inability to articulate what I feel or see. I am afraid, Jim, of what I may not be able to do, of what I may not be able to accomplish, and so that irritation sometimes leads me to despair of my limited abilities. But this particular day, because I had just been stung by something terribly painful (a scorpion I never saw, resting on a bag of horse feed), I could easily blame the sting for somehow interfering with my concentration on the cloud. But the truth is, stung or not, I couldn't manage that one white cloud. One of the red birds that came up from Mexico to eat saguaro fruits and prickly pears reminded me of the swirled reds and whites of clouds at sunset, but later I thought it was just an excess of imagination on my part, the impulse to describe birds that way. Then one evening the sky was exactly that color of the bird's feathers, and I was a little frightened of myself.

When I was a little girl and we lost a beloved dog or cat, often strays which people dumped out along Highway 66 would come to us. My father always told us that these strays knew we had just lost a cat or dog and that's why they came. It was a little strange how that used to happen, but coincidence is what you'd have to call it. Anyway, lately, there has been a roadrunner coming around the house. I remember him last year when we still had the rooster, but the roadrunner was much more shy then and used to hurry away. Well, little by little this roadrunner has learned he can come around and the dogs won't harm him. He likes to jump up on the hoods of cars and trucks and he snoops around in the back of our truck and steals pieces of paper or rags he finds. I know he thinks these things are valuable because he runs like a thief down the road when he takes them. The speckled cactus wren scolds him whenever he comes around – I almost know when I will find him by the sounds of the wrens. This morning he jumped on the ledge of our bedroom window and was looking inside with the same expression in his little crazed eyes that rooster used to have, though the roadrunner seems more determinedly curious and audacious than rooster ever was – I suppose because rooster was domesticated a little.

PART 2

Aunt Susie's clan is the Roadrunner clan, and Lucy Lewis who paints the beautiful running deer on her Acoma pots, she too is from the Roadrunner clan. Anyway, I am happy to see this roadrunner around the house and have decided this might be the best sort of "pet" to have, because the coyotes will have a difficult time with him. The people at home never thought of the animals like roadrunners or coyotes in the way that Americans think of their "pets"–they sort of thought of them as equals, or kinspeople you could get angry with and yell at, or living beings you could feel companionship with. There is a big diamondback that comes around our corrals and feed barn (where the mean little scorpions lurk) to hunt the mice and pack rats which are really out of control this season. He (I decided this because he is so unassuming and gentle without nesting to occupy him) was curled up in the pile of cement blocks by the hay barn when I moved an old piece of tin and saw his beautiful black and white pattern. He's so fat this year that he is even less inclined to coil or rattle, and when we took a stick to move him carefully to a less hazardous place he would not even strike at the stick. I named him "Baby" although he is four feet long and as big around as my lower arm. I would much rather have Baby in the hay barn than these mean little scorpions who are very aggressive and difficult to see, but I know that he will move along as soon as the mice population is somewhat reduced and we won't see him until next year when the mice are again out of hand.

Just this afternoon we saw a gila monster crossing the highway about 3 miles from the house. It was the first time I've ever seen one that wasn't in the zoo. We backed up the truck to look at it and it lumbered down the shoulder of the road but in a semi-circle because, as Robert pointed out, it still intended to cross the road even if we had driven by and temporarily turned it back. It was pinkish-orange and black–the orange was almost identical to the sand and rock in the area where we saw it. I always thought I wouldn't like gila monsters because in the glass cases in the zoos they look so pudgy and lethargic, but this one today had a way of traveling that made me like him at once–he wasn't fast or graceful like other lizards but he was determined and brave crossing the pavement. His tail reserves of fat were modest too, and I realized that moving as slowly as he does, catching his meals is probably much more of a chore than the books and films about desert animals would have you believe about gila monsters.

Forgive me for writing so much about desert animals this time. I had intended to tell you a little about a new story I am working on, but it might be better simply to send you a draft when I get it finished. On the 26th of August I go to New Mexico to begin the semester (I will teach a single advanced fiction course from Tucson with occasional visits to the class in Albuquerque throughout the semester) and then on the 1st I will be at the English Institute meeting at Harvard to say something about Native American views of language and the use of English. But after that I will be here in Tucson, and I am so much looking forward to spending the coming weeks and months of the fall with my poor neglected writing projects.

I would feel so fortunate to see any of the new poems, Jim, but don't go to any trouble please. I hope you and Annie are having a pleasurable visit in Paris. I don't know Sisley's work but am determined to find it at the University of Arizona library. I appreciate so much hearing from you, Jim. Thank you for being here now.

Love,
Leslie

❀

Paris, France
August 23, 1979

Dear Leslie,

We plan to leave Paris for New York on September 4th. Today is August 23rd. I may write to you again before we leave. I don't know.

Something tells me that at this time of year you may well be very busy. And you have given me so much during the last eight months (and longer, about a year) that I am afraid I might sound demanding, but I will ask you anyway: would you be kind enough to write to me in New York? The address there is as follows: 529 East 85th Street, New York, N.Y. 10028. This European journey has been a long one and, in spite of the beauty of Paris, I am ready to come home. Even so, New York will be a kind of shock, as it always is. It would make me happy to have a letter from you there when I arrive.

I've spent this morning typing out six pieces to send to you.* I wrote all of them here in Europe, and all except one (the piece about the sumac tree) are going to be published soon, in various places. I chose these six out of about forty that I've completed, and I send them to you out of gratitude for the inspiration that your friendship never fails to provide. Our correspondence is one of the finest things I have ever had anything to do with in my life, and I trust it will continue.

Paris in August is mostly a gray city, but when the clouds open they reveal a sky most remarkably blue, even more thrilling in its depth than the nearly incomparable skies over Hawaii. As I write these words, the sky is just opening.

It gives me great joy to know that your new book will be appearing soon. I am working on two: some poems, and a book of essays. Neither is finished, not by a long shot. But I got a lot of work done this last few months, and I ought to be satisfied. (I'm not, of course.)

Now I'll try to get this into the mail.

With love,
Jim

*The six pieces were: "Wherever Home Is," "Leave Him Alone," "A Dark Moor Bird," "The Vestal in the Forum," "Entering the Temple at Nimes," "The Sumac in Ohio."

New York, N.Y.
September 7, 1979

Dear Leslie,

We are home in New York, and this is going to be a short note. In less than fifteen minutes I've got to get hopping further already, and take the train down to Hunter College, where I've got all sorts of practical jobs planned for myself. After this long year of working on another kind of thing – rather, working in another manner – I am eager to focus my attention in a slightly different way. What it means is that I have got to contend with and deal with people in the ruck and tumble of New York. It is a life I sought, all right, and in many ways I like it. But it is different from sitting for solitary hours with my notebook and then leisurely prowling the ancient deserted streets of, say, Carcassonne, where we walked all day in a rainy fog. I don't really think that Carcassonne was deserted, and I had a full sense, really, of the people who had lived there, the vividness of their lives, the strange and sometimes funny things they did as they lived out their days in this world. But in New York, people are living out their days too, and I am living out mine with them. It is clutter, clutter, clutter, and I have to find my way through it.

By this time you ought to be home, and I am really writing to greet you and to let you know I am thinking of you and your place and work. I have some other things to tell you, but they will have to wait for a few days, till I have marked out my path here.

I hope your trip to Harvard was a success. I read a paper at the English Institute years ago (on Whitman), and sometime this fall I am supposed to speak at Harvard again. But that is one of the cluttering arrangements that, as I mentioned, I have to make.

I feel pretty good, and I hope you do too, my dear friend. Please write me here when you can.

Love,
Jim

❦

Tucson, Arizona
September 12, 1979

Dear Jim,

The poems you sent were so filled with your special wonder and the sound of peace you find in evening light, I wanted surely to have a letter waiting for you when you reached New York. But like the lizard, I didn't. If I couldn't have the time I needed for a letter to you, then I wouldn't write. I think I trust your understanding in this. I don't think anyone – no American – has ever written like you do, has ever written this American language like you do. You are fearless of the language America speaks and you love it. Some I think did not or do not fear it, but they do not love it and so write an English we seldom hear outside the university; and then there are many who love it but are afraid it isn't "poetic" or "literary." You bring such grace and delicacy from it, coax out the astonishing range of dissonances and harmonies it allows us, that with your poems behind me I can speak confidently now about a beauty which is purely from the American heart.

When I say "American" language I mean it in the widest sense – with the expansiveness of spirit which the great land and many peoples allow. No need ever to have limited it to so few sensibilities, so few visions of what there might be in this world. At the English Institute many of the members seemed so reluctant to acknowledge that Jamaican poets are using an

English language which at once loves the music of the language so much as it loves the people and the life which speak the language. It seemed that the English Institute people have somehow "forgotten" what Shakespeare loved most and did best – created moments of powerful, overwhelming vision, but with the language the people *spoke*, not wrote. When I think of all the puns and jokes and political jibes Shakespeare worked into his plays – all because he was conscious of the "street" English used both by the common people and by the upper classes when they "went into the streets" either literally or figuratively – and then think of the English Institute growing uncomfortable at the idea that Native American English does exist – well, Jim, I think you get the point. I dislike even to label it "Native American" and would like to think that we could see language more flexible and inclusive, that we could begin to look for the passion and the expression instead of language by rote. Television English in these past 10 or 15 years – that hideous, empty, artificial language television speaks – is the result of the past 50 years of working to eradicate regional usages, regional pronunciations, i.e., regional and community expression from American English, always with the melting pot theory in mind. To have a "standardized" language, in a land as big and as geographically diverse as this, certainly seems ridiculous to me. Pre-Columbian America had hundreds and hundreds – maybe thousands – of completely distinct language groups. Even with the Pueblo people who shared such similar views of the world and similar geographies there are/were tremendous differences.

That is what I love most in your writing, Jim, the gully and railroad track, the sumac and coal smoke – all could only be from the place you give us or that gives you to us, that Ohio country. That Ohio country gives us your voice in "Wherever Home Is" so that you can say "Good-bye to Leonardo, good riddance" and "I'm going home with the lizard" – because that's how it sounds in you from Ohio where you come from.

Well, I didn't mean to go on like that so much. I doubt that you need to read such stuff as this when you are back in the city and very busy.

I am busy with details on the film script project but also am beginning to be able to sort out details of my future. For example, I don't think that I will be able to keep my position at the University of New Mexico much longer, simply because it does not allow me the time or flexibility to do the work I need to do. University rules allow researchers in lasers and atomic reactors to spend years and years away from students, but a person in the arts or humanities is allowed only one year for projects. Of course the U. of N.M. is one institution which could not exist except for the Federal money it receives from the Atomic Energy Commission and the Defense Department. So better that I find some other way to buy tennis shoes for Robert and rolled barley for the mares.

I am waiting for the rain which has been flirtatious and coy. Yesterday 12 drops fell and then the clouds moved around Wasson Peak and were gone. I hung up wet laundry and took a long walk and threw dry alfalfa to the horses – all acts calculated to make it rain. But it isn't that easy; it never was.

Grandma Lillie's heart trouble is getting worse, and I suppose it will be just so much longer and then she will be gone. When I was home at the end of August she sat up late and listened to me talk about the things I was doing. I thought it a little strange because I never think she will be interested, but she is. Sometimes I feel I want to be with her now, but I know that what she likes is for a person to be busy with the things which need to be done – she always has. That's how I am sometimes, wondering if I am where I should be, at the time when I should be.

I promise you an altogether better letter next time, Jim.

Love,
Leslie

New York, N.Y.
September 18, 1979

Dear Leslie,

Thanks so much for your long letter. Your reflections on language really helped me as I was thinking about the matter and trying to introduce my students, especially my freshmen, to the task we're undertaking this semester. I want them to learn how to write a clear and direct prose that will have a certain formality, a certain clear dignity, without their sacrificing their sense of themselves. What you say about Native American and its variety is beautiful and I am convinced it is still the heart of what we are trying, those of us who care about the language and living voices, to do in this country.

I think you would enjoy my students, as I do. I'm sure you've been to New York several times, and probably you have the same horrified impression that I often still have. And yet there is something remarkably fine here, and it is to be found in its best form and in the most immediate way among my students at a place like Hunter. Perhaps as recently as twenty-five years ago, Hunter was a college entirely for women. They were all white and middle-class, and the school itself was rather exclusive. I don't mean to sneer at it. On the contrary, Hunter earned the reputation of being one of the best colleges in the United States. Then things changed, and we all went through the same kind of transition everyone else was going through. It took many forms, but, to me, what it means – what it still means, in fact because we're still in the midst of it – is that whole large groups of people emerged, suddenly and finally and irrevocably, into the mainstream, the main consciousness, of American life. At Hunter, this means that my students come from a quite fantastic and rich variety of backgrounds. I literally have students who come, or whose families come, from everywhere: Jamaica, Haiti, Trinidad, Russia, Poland, Israel, Egypt, Palestine (yes, indeed) and all over the United States. For a while, this was confusing, as it had to be. Now, I am discovering, again and again, wonderful intelligences expressed through an incredibly rich rhythm of language.... But the work, as always at first, is hard, time-consuming. I know what you mean about the New Mexico job. Somehow, so far, I've been able to keep my notebook going. Forgive this too-brief note. We'll settle down.

Love,
Jim

❦

Tucson, Arizona
October 14, 1979

Dear Jim,

Typing today on this letter reminds me only of how much time has passed since I last wrote to you and how many chores I've still got to attend to before November 15th. I know you are just as busy yourself, and yet you still manage to write to me.

I am working with the other three cycles of stories to be covered in the N.E.H. film project which includes the Estoyehmuut story – I love the stories so much that just working with them gives me great pleasure. Sometimes I don't even do much toward getting them into a script "treatment" form like I am supposed to be doing: sometimes I just work with them and the ways of telling them over and over again. I keep running across all the different versions of single stories which Aunt Susie has told – even as I type "single" stories or think "same story" I realize that I am learning now that there is no such thing, that every time she told a story and told it like it was the only version, well, it *was* the only version of *that* story; and it is just a certain training we have, a training that makes us want to group ideas or stories together, which leads us to want to or try to lump together all the stories, calling them "versions" of the same story. I mean, I guess, that is one way of thinking about them. But I am learning that this is *not* the way Aunt Susie or the old-timers felt when they were doing the telling – there actually is "the story" which people hear and tell, with different details, according to how their family or village tells it. But there is also another sense of the story, and that is "the story" of a particular telling (as with music, I suppose), the story that will never again be told in quite the same way with quite the same context.

I don't know why I am so intrigued with this – perhaps because it seems a way of understanding the dynamics of change and changing and how some elements seem to come through "change" without themselves having lost certain characteristics.

Sometimes it is Antelope who butts a hole through the earth so that the people can find their way out of the underworld into this world: and so the people of the Antelope clan figure they get to be first in all the earthly ceremonies since then; but Aunt Susie has an even finer story of how Antelope strikes the earth with his head and paws at it with his hooves but only manages to make a small hole, too small for the emergence. And it is then that Badger comes forth and uses his claws and works very patiently scratching and digging until he makes the hole through which all the people emerge. Lately I found an account which Aunt Susie told in 1936, though she *did* say (she was telling it to her daughter Miriam who wrote it down) that it was her clansman, Paul Johnson's, story. (Right there we have the reason it is so different from the ones I heard from her.) Anyway, in this story, Arrowboy shoots an arrow through the earth and makes the hole that was needed. I say the Badger story seems "finer" to me, but that is just a personal preference; what seems to be more and more clear is that each version is true and each version is correct and what matters is to have as many of the stories as possible and to have them together and to understand the emergence, keeping all the stories in mind at the same time. At least this is how it seems to me right now.

You know, Jim, sometimes I feel *almost* like I can begin to see (or maybe "sense" is a better word for it) the way the ancient Pueblo people viewed the world and happenings in the world. Maybe they saw the world and happenings in it the way David Hume posited or in a way that is close to Hume's at least insofar as "happenings" or experience are concerned. I think of how old movies made fun of "primitive" people who feared the loss of sun at winter solstice or at eclipse time. But it is "true" that the time will come when this sun in this solar system will pass from existence, when simply because the sun has risen and been with the earth for millions and millions or billions of years does not mean that it will always be so.

It seems that the old old ones took nothing for granted, at least not the rising of the sun. And that they did not limit experience to "single episodes at single times." It must have been that any number of things could be happening at the same place at the same time, so to speak. Whose "parallel paths," I wonder? Is that Berkeley? I wish I knew more about Western thought. Well, so much for Antelope, Badger and Arrowboy.

Storyteller is with Viking's designers, and who knows how long it will take – because the photographs are to be related to the text in precise ways, which means the designers have little latitude with the arranging. It seems to take longer and longer for a book to become a "book." I suppose that it won't be out until next winter. Anyway, my big writing concern now is the film project and finishing it up. I am happy to have *Storyteller* in the works even if it really isn't a "big piece," like *Ceremony* was. I think that putting it together gave me a great deal – that

I discovered a great deal in making *Storyteller*. I think it is the book I was worried about, the book I felt I should do; the night before I had the emergency surgery almost three years ago now, my greatest and I think my *only* regret about my life was that I hadn't yet written all the stories that needed writing. Anyway, Jim, this book removes that burden.

I have told the U. of N.M. that I cannot teach this coming spring. So I will be here for sure when you and Annie come to Tucson. I hope you can spend at least one night here with us to listen to the coyotes. I know the Poetry Center will have all your time allotted, but I hope we can find at least one evening here. We have plenty of space and privacy to offer.

Meanwhile back at the ranch the cistern is low because this is a hot, dry fall with winds that move the clouds too quickly past us, and I am allowing every kind of chore to pile up, telling everything it must "wait" until I finish this film project. Never again film projects, Jim, that's what I say.

I hope you and Annie are both feeling well and enjoying the autumn in New York – beautiful, I bet.

Take care,
Love,
Leslie

New York, N.Y.
October 20, 1979

Dear Leslie,

I'm especially happy to hear from you – come to think of it, your letters always give me a sense of happiness, even when you speak of difficult and painful things, because you always give me the sense of flourishing no matter what, of somehow keeping in touch with your real life.

Having said this much, however, I confess that I've been wondering about your present condition, the circumstances under which you are living and working, and your plans for the next year or few years. What I am talking about is probably (no, certainly) a violation of your privacy, a curiosity that is plain rudeness however one looks at it; and I hope very much, and somewhat perilously, that you won't be offended by my indelicate nosiness. This is all just a polite way of saying that I've been wondering how you're going to make a living in the absence of that job in New Mexico and in the process of your writing. Now my situation is different. I am a teacher by profession. I am a Ph.D. in English Literature, a Full Professor (don't you love the capitalization?) of English at Hunter College of the City University of New York. I have tenure; so it is unlikely that I will be fired unless I get so drunk I ignore my classes entirely or else perform an unnatural act with a badger in such a way as to obstruct rush-hour traffic: and I don't drink at all (a real teetotaler), and I'm too old to badger. The books I write are, I trust, serious, at least I want them to be serious; but they are, realistically speaking, avocations. Moreover, all of my writings are short: verses, essays, descriptive prose pieces. But I read your superb outline for the novel about Geronimo, and I know perfectly well that the writing of such a book will be a full-time job, as *Ceremony* undoubtedly was. This is why I've been wondering about your situation (I trust my other reason goes without saying). I am assuming that the Guggenheim didn't work (I hope, by the way, that you're going to apply again, and I hope you'll let me write them another letter)....I loved all that you wrote this time about the stories, and your Aunt Susie sounds like one of the greatest of people. Annie and I are both well, working hard. We will definitely be in

Tucson next spring between Saturday, March 29th and Sunday, April 6th. We will *love* to stay overnight with you.

Love,
Jim

❦

Tucson, Arizona
November 5, 1979

Dear Jim,

Please forgive the messy manuscript I've sent* but I don't have time to arrange for a typist and if I do it, I just keep fussing with the story until I squeeze the life out of it.

This is the story I told you I was working with in early August. It tried to become a novel during the second draft, but, after a week of fighting with it, I managed to determine that it *should be* a *story*. It was still resisting, so I put all the drafts (4 or 5) and notes in a folder and threw it in a box. In years past, it might never have been finished. Many of my "unfinished" stories unexpectedly materialized in *Ceremony*, so I don't fret over unfinished stories. I have a naïve faith that somehow, at some time, all the stories in me will get told. I'm very excited that I was able to pick up the story again and finish it as I'd originally wanted it. I hope this is a sign of a new "steadfastness" and maturity on my part. I hope this means I am learning how to write fiction even when I don't have large expanses of time and calm in my life. I've been sort of "mule-ish" these past years, not writing longer fiction pieces because the conditions didn't suit me. But I guess I finally realized that if I wait

*A typewritten copy of the short story "Coyote Sits with a Full House in His Hand" was enclosed with this letter. It is part of the book *Storyteller*.

for large expanses of time and peace, I'll never write longer fiction again.

Money buys large expanses of time: I recently had a "run-in" with a poet who heads the writing program at Arizona State University in Tempe. He was bothered because I expressed concern over money. He seemed to prefer the idea of writing regardless of finances – sort of a romantic notion – like painters eating crackers so they can buy tubes of cadmium blue. Now, Jim, I can write just about anything under just about any circumstances, but there is a certain vein that my longer fiction runs in, and when I'm teaching or have other schedules to keep, that vein sort of hides itself. It *won't* come out until the bill collectors are gone and until there are no more student manuscripts waiting. I suspect this means that in "this day" long fiction is doomed, because we no longer can afford to allow anyone, even fine fiction writers, the luxuries of time and peace that long fiction demands. Maybe writing (and reading) long fiction is decadent. Do you suppose? I love doing nothing but writing – I steal time from chores and duties as much as my poor conscience allows (I can't seem to ignore the needs of people very well, so I'm not much good except to ignore dirty clothes and holes in the roof, and if *people* complain about the holes or clothes, then I hop to and attend to them).

I'm on salary from the University of New Mexico until December 15th and then I'll be back to depending on readings and technical writing work I do for some Indian lawyers. U. of N.M. expects me to have 40 students *writing* each semester, plus one lecture class in literature once a year or 2 classes in fall and 3 classes in spring. I work with the student fiction word by word, so it means an almost impossible task with 40 students. So although the finances are precarious, my writing is better when I *don't* teach. *Ceremony* paid fairly well while it was in hard cover, but in paper it brings about $1,700 per year. The new book, *Storyteller*, won't do as well because it isn't a novel.

I decided to wait for *Storyteller* before applying for a Guggenheim again – anyway, I got too busy this year to bother with it – but I will certainly do it *next* year.

I seem to manage somehow, so far, Jim.

Robert's father sends $100 now instead of $25 per month, and Robert's grandparents help me buy his shoes and clothes. Anyway, I have horses and old Navajo rugs to sell before I run out of typing paper.

Everything is going along okay. I feel so much better after I write a story. I'm a slow writer and haven't *ever* been prolific, although my excuse has always been too little time. They say you'll *make the time*, but do "they" have kids, leaky roofs, broken-down cars and telephone bills? The way I see it, Jim, is I'll have to get thrown in jail to "make the time." Of course with my luck I'd go to a jail where they make you work in the laundry all day long.

Sorry to go on and on, but it's so seldom I get to escape into a letter to you.

Let me know what you think of the story – just how much you laughed or yawned – I don't need any more than that, and you're busy yourself. Take care of yourself. Hello to Annie.

Love,
Leslie

❧

New York, N.Y.
November 18, 1979

Dear Leslie,

"Coyote Holds a Full House in His Hand" is rapidly and cleanly written, and it is (therefore) very funny. I think it is important that episodes like this be short enough to give a reader or a listener (come to think of it, I felt as much like a listener as a reader of this story) a chance to let his mind fly out into that extra, larger dimension that a real comedy offers. It's hard to get my thoughts about this matter clearly down on paper. When I say "short" I don't mean just in bulk.

I know something about Coyote, but not enough. Still, I'm sure I grasped the story. It is fine.

I am happy that in the midst of everything you are able to keep working. If that makes you stubborn, then the hell with it, you're stubborn. You know, Leslie, for a while during the past weeks I've feared that my sense of being too busy, or being harassed by the demands of the world, was just personal neurosis. But now I'm becoming aware that most of the people I know – and not just New Yorkers, either – feel harassed in the same way. Everybody seems in danger of being suffocated by busywork. I wonder what it all means. I have been struggling hard: I get up, usually at 5:30 a.m., and study for a couple of hours before I go to teach. After teaching for three or four hours, depending on the day, I go to my office and work a couple more hours on paperwork for school. When I get home I am truly exhausted, so I close my eyes for an hour or less. Then I rise and write in my notebook. I have never failed to do this, but I certainly feel driven.

I want to thank you for taking my last letter in such a friendly way, and for replying in clear detail. At the moment I'm not sure what I can do to help, but I am glad (it sounds like an odd word, but I am glad) to have a clearer notion of just how you're doing and just how (really too little) much money you have coming in. I'm a good deal older than you, and I know something about this particular kind of struggle.

I miss you – again, an odd thought, since we've never really met. But we will. Please write when you can.

Love,
Jim

Tucson, Arizona
December 12, 1979

Dear Jim,

Please don't give up on me – I've been composing letters to you these past weeks while I wash dirty clothes, sweep, and dig out my desk from under the papers. It is the aftermath of the N.E.H. proposal work, when I had to let everything take care of itself. But the proposal was sent in to N.E.H. on time, and with some luck we may have funding for the Estoyehmuut film by April 1st.

Today is our first day of cold damp weather, but we need the rain and today we only got a short rainstorm. It has been so dry that the fillies raise great clouds of dust when they play in the corral. The sorrel filly even got bronchitis from the dry air and dust. The rabbits are chewing the lower stems and the pads of the prickly pears because there's nothing else for them. Still the desert looks good – the dryness is nothing unusual and the rains are about on time.

I'm knitting mittens and caps for my nieces – the knitting soothes me, and my sisters both live in cold climates where such things are needed. I'm not very good at dealing with Christmas so far as advance preparations are concerned, but this year I *am* trying. We'll go up to Gallup and have Christmas with my mother. Caz will be with us. I'm very much looking forward to this time with him. He was to have come to Tucson on November 15th, but got an ear infection. The doctor gave him a long-acting shot of penicillin and two weeks later, when I was over in Albuquerque to teach my class, I noticed Caz had hives. It got much worse and as it turns out, Caz is allergic to the drug. I took him to the doctor and spent as much time with him as I could. He didn't feel terribly bad, but his eyes were swollen shut and his lips swelled out like a pie pony.

Robert is having a difficult time being 13. I think he's "young" for his age, but because he is physically mature, his peers expect him to give up his games and fantasy worlds for more practical concerns like football and girl friends. And being away from his brother and from his stepfather is difficult too. Anyway, lately I've been trying to help him work out his bad headaches and the eczema on his face – which means many trips from the ranch to town and the doctors.

After the holidays I hope I will be able to get back to my own work. I'd like to do another story like the Coyote story I sent to you. I'm not sure, Jim, if I understand the difficulty you found with the story. I hope we can talk about it when you come. My interest is in what allows us to laugh at stories which are not altogether funny in and of themselves, but become funny when people begin to recall and tell other stories about related incidents. This happens a lot at Laguna with stories about funerals, and I know in other places, humor's link with the most grave and serious moments has always been acknowledged. Anyhow the Coyote story was my first attempt, and I'll keep wrestling with it.

I got a call from a woman at the Manhattan Theatre Club, and Peter Matthiessen, whom I've never met, has asked that I read with him on February 5th. If I can find another reading in New York City to help cover the plane fare then perhaps I'll see you *before* you and Annie come to Tucson. I did a number of readings in New York last January so I don't expect to have much luck. Mei-Mei is usually in New York then, and it's so tempting to go when I have the excuse of a reading. Still, I just did my little notebook for my income tax records, and I've got to be more careful about these whimsical flights to New York.

Please forgive the mess my printing and spelling are tonight. Sometimes I have spells when I transpose letters and whole words and cannot see at all that I've done it.

My typewriter is in the front bedroom and it's too cold to

sit in there. I'm worse though with the machine when I have these spells.

I hope you and Annie will have a happy holiday time. I think of you often even if I don't write.

Love,
Leslie

❦

New York, N.Y.
December 18, 1979

Dear Leslie,

I'm afraid this will be a short note for the moment – I'll write at greater length later on. I have some bad news about myself which I nevertheless want to tell you.

I have learned that I have cancer. It is very serious, but it is not hopeless. My doctor is a good man and a highly skilled specialist, and he has assured me and Annie that the operation – radical surgery in the throat – will save my life. I will emerge from the surgery with diminished capacity to speak, and this will create a problem, since I make a living by speaking. But there is a good chance that I will be able to continue teaching all right. The operation is supposed to take place early in the month of January. I will be recuperating here at home most of the time. Because the operation will be serious and debilitating, I have arranged to take off the spring semester from teaching.

It is a shock, of course, perhaps the most cruel shock that a middle-aged person can face. But I have found that I have a number of considerable powers to help me. I have always been happy with my marriage to Annie, for example, but I suddenly have a deeper and clearer understanding of how very strong this marriage is. Furthermore, in determining who to tell, I have considered that I want to share the worst of this news with a very few people whom I admire and value the most, and it is interesting to me that you stand very high in my mind among those – the people, I mean, who strike me as embodying in their own lives and work something – some value, some spirit – that I absolutely care about and believe in. Of course, my dear friend, over little more than a year we have become excellent friends, and I would hope always to send you happy news. But the tragic news belongs to you too. Please don't despair over my troubles. I will find my way through this difficulty somehow, and one of the best things I have is my knowledge that you exist and that you are going on living and working. I'll be in touch again soon (by the way, if you're in N.Y.C. on February 5th please *do* call us.

Love,
Jim

❖

Tucson, Arizona
January 3, 1980

Dear Jim,

Your letter was waiting when I returned from Christmas in Gallup. I wanted to wait a few days to digest it in case my feelings changed, but they have not and I trust them. I feel a great deal of distress about your speaking voice because I imagine how you must be feeling about it; but myself, I have always felt that the words and the feeling they were spoken with matter most, and I sense that this is your deepest understanding too, otherwise your letter would not have been so calm. When I was a girl my grandpa on my mother's side had just the same operation. In those days they didn't have the electronic mechanisms they have now. But all my memories of him are of his expressiveness, which I did not perceive before, although I was younger before, and maybe this is the reason. He smiled and gestured a lot and like always, he would cry when he was very happy – he was often overcome with feelings, and my mother is the same, and I am too. We can be in an airport or train depot not even seeing anyone off and when they call the train or plane, we cry. I don't know what or who we cry for, but we do. Grandpa was always that way, but after the operation it always seemed to me much more a way of speaking than simply some overflow of feeling. I suppose it is because of this and because the operation was successful for him that I read your letter calmly. Perhaps I am seeing your crisis too much like a child, and perhaps this confidence that you will be here for quite some time is my way of protecting myself from pain, but I think not. I know such things immediately; the feeling hits me and I'm never able to think fast enough to create a rationalization. I feel you will be all right, that your health will be restored. You will manage the part about your voice because voice never was sound alone. Which doesn't mean that you won't feel angry sometimes – Grandpa did, but then he learned his own new language.

I know all the stories which are told at times like these – I suppose I hesitate because there is a sort of cultural context in which they exist and New York now must be even more distant from it. Or maybe not.

It seems strange how some people get far more than their fair share of illness or trouble. I suppose Spinoza would say that Existence never heard of "fair." Hugh Crooks came to Laguna in the 1920s from somewhere in the East or Midwest. He was in his early 20s and his doctors sent him to the Southwest with tuberculosis so bad they told him just to plan on spending his last months in New Mexico. He came and waited and then nothing happened so he got a job running the store for Abie Abraham there at Laguna (this was before my Grandpa Hank had the store). My dad remembers Hugh then, always in a short-sleeved shirt even when it was snowing, and always coughing, always real skinny. My dad was just a mean little kid then, and one time he set fire to the boxes of paper and trash by the back door of the store Hugh was managing for Abie. My dad hid on the big hill north of Laguna and looked down and watched Hugh carry buckets of water to put out the fire. It seemed like Hugh never got over the t.b., but the years went by, and the next thing that happened was a terrible car wreck. Hugh was driving down the old road to Los Lunas and collided with a truck. People from Laguna who happened to drive past reported that it was all over for Hugh – I remember the graphic description – they said his pelvic bones were shoved clear up to his armpits, though that sounds a lot like embroidery. But no, he recovered in time, and the years went by, and I think he liked to drink a lot. I don't remember hearing much about Hugh other than this litany which I am reciting to you, Jim, this litany of his physical disasters. I think now that there wasn't much that was remarkable about Hugh otherwise – he wasn't a mean man and he didn't cheat people, but I think he had a pretty ordinary life except for these terrible illnesses and accidents for which we have always known him. Anyway, I guess he did some drinking, though it was never the sort that led to broken screen doors or fights. He never married, and it wasn't until many many years later that my mother figured out why that might have been. Anyway, the next thing we knew, someone had been to the hospital to see Hugh, and this time it was his liver and they said Hugh won't make it this time, his liver is swollen up as big as a watermelon, and everyone went to visit him thinking that this was it. Aunt Florence went to see him, and Aunt Mary, and they both said that it was true that he had survived the t.b. and the car wreck but this time the cirrhosis had him. Well everybody said it was too bad, but after all it was lucky he had lived this long, and that it was funny too that one or two of the people who had seen him in the wreckage of his truck and pronounced him a goner – well, they were gone by this time, in one way or another. But this time... Hugh got out of the hospital and was back in his pickup truck driving around, still smoking, still coughing, in his short-sleeved shirts. Pretty soon he was running a bar at Swanee, which is where old U.S. 66 used to intersect the old highway to Los Lunas. Swanee is just off the Laguna reservation and near the Navajo reservation land at Cañoncito. Anyway, the bar was always busy with Lagunas and Navajos buying liquor and with passersby on U.S. 66 and the Los Lunas road. Hugh liked keeping the bar pretty well because he liked talking to people and he liked his regular customers, and I guess he liked being able to drink some himself too. I think he wasn't very ambitious and he never seemed like he had much money or cared whether he did. Anyway, one night some hold-up men passing through on 66 held up Hugh's bar (crooks traveling on Highway 66 from Chicago to L.A. or vice versa used to run out of money right around the Laguna area and then they'd break in or do a hold-up). Hugh took out a .38 he kept under the counter and shot one of the hold-up men (didn't kill him), but then the other shot Hugh in the chest with a .38. He was in critical condition for a long time, and then just when he was getting better he got pneumonia, and the doctors (doctors who knew Hugh also knew better than to say anything but these doctors didn't know and so they) said he wouldn't pull through. All Grandpa Hank would say was "I wonder if Hugh will make it this time," and he did; and it was right after this that my mom was driving to Albuquerque on Highway 66 and she saw Hugh picking up a young hitchhiker, and then coming home she saw him on the other side of the highway picking up another hitchhiker (he wasn't running the bar any more), and that was when we got some idea maybe about Hugh and his life and why he wasn't married and why he had friends like my mom and my aunts who were women, but no girl friends to speak of. Not long after this, my Grandpa Hank died and Hugh came to the funeral, and someone made the remark later that it was funny how Hugh was still going long after many of the people who had always expected Hugh to die before they did.

I don't think Grandpa Hank thought this, but a lot of others did. Aunt Florence was already gone by then too, now that I think of it, and she had been *so sure* that time Hugh had the liver trouble. By this time now it had become pretty clear to all of us, but when Hugh went into the hospital for cancer of the gums, Aunt Lorena and Aunt Mary saw him and reported that this *absolutely was it* for Hugh, and they stood their ground when Grandma Lillee and my dad reminded them of the people who had said that before and who were gone. Somewhere during this time too there was some mention of Hugh's liver and cancer, so maybe that's why as Aunt Lorena was driving to Mass with her little granddaughter in Los Lunas she had a stroke and was gone. A year or so later, Aunt Mary got one of her asthma attacks and didn't recover. Hugh Crooks is almost eighty now. It's my dad's generation and mine (and a lot of my dad's generation are gone now too) – we who grew up in awe of Hugh because the adults around us were always talking about him being on his last legs – it's we now who are left, and of course time changes perspectives. We got to know something which the older people didn't because they didn't have the benefit of time. Yet beyond this simple parable level I'm not sure what this story means.

But I like the story because there's this humor in it right along and it intrigues me that there is this man who is known almost solely for the simple fact that he is alive. When I think I'm getting more than my fair share of trouble I always remember Hugh Crooks stories or Harry Marmon stories (Harry got out of the physical ones unscathed, but there were always jail and police and lawyers and fines, and still Harry is a free man). Maybe if a person can manage way more than his or her fair share of trouble, then another sort of perspective or dimension is involved, I don't know. At Laguna they say it just makes you tougher. In the old days even where there was plenty of food they'd all practice for famine – it wasn't puritanical or Calvinistic at all – it was simply practical to make yourself tough enough, because famine is inevitable.

Today, Jim, I am going to work on my garden plot. I hope to grow a few snow peas, some spinach, and some sweet peas. I will be happy just with sweet peas which do very well down here in the winter and early spring. I have chosen a place about 20 feet below the drain for the kithen sink water and will grow these crops with dishwater. We've had no winter yet to speak of and having a garden will make me very happy.

You are a dear dear friend, Jim. In so many ways it was you who helped me through those difficult times last year. At times like these I often wish I had more to say, but somehow it comes out in a story. I hope all this does not strike you as too strange. I seem not to react like most people do at times like these. I think I sense your calm and your deep faith. I know it has to do with your wonderful writing and, more important, with the visions that emerge from it.

Love,
Leslie

❁

James Wright was hospitalized in mid-January 1980 with cancer of the tongue, diagnosed upon hospital entry as terminal. He was able to read Leslie's letter of January 3rd before he was too ill to remain in his home.

Leslie came to speak at the Manhattan Theatre Club in New York on

February 5th. On the following day I arrived at the hospital after work to find Leslie sitting by James's bedside. Although unable to speak, James did respond to Leslie's conversation by writing on a yellow-lined legal pad.

He wrote this about the people who cared for him: "People are lovely to me here. Mr. Edwards and Mrs. Holmes are amazing, understanding, companions. They are skilled and I trust them."

Later that evening, after Leslie had gone, James wrote me a note about her visit. "I have the sense of a very fine, great person—a true beautiful artist. And I'm glad we've all made friends."

In March James and I wrote a post card to Leslie together. It was the only thing he wrote while in the hospital.

This is the message we wrote together from the hospital.

Dear Leslie,

I can't write much of a message. Please write to me.

Love,
Jim

We loved seeing you last month. James is moving to a fine new hospital on Friday.*

We miss hearing from you. How is the roadrunner?

Love,
Annie

*Calvary Hospital in the Bronx.

[Leslie's last letter to James, dated March 24th, arrived after his death.]

Tucson, Arizona
March 24, 1980

Dear Jim,

I have been trusting another sort of communication between you and me – a sort of message from the heart – sent by thinking of you and feeling great love for you and knowing strongly that you think of me, that you are sending thoughts and feelings to me; and you and I, Jim, we *trust* in these messages that move between us.

I cannot account for this except that perhaps it is a gift of the poetry, or perhaps it should be called "grace" – a special sort of grace. I am never far from you, Jim, and this feeling I have knows that we will never be far from each other, you and I. Aunt Susie has taught me this much and my Grandpa Hank and Great-Grandma have too – that knowing and loving someone has no end, and that we are together always, over at the Cliff House or walking along the lake edge not far from the home Catullus keeps.

It is not easy to avoid confusion. What I wanted to do was stay in New York, move in with Annie, and sit with you and talk with you. But that would have been confusing one present time with another present time.

Anyway, I know you understand, Jim, and I know Annie does too.

In one present time, you and I can count the times we've met and the minutes we've actually spent together. I think I was very shy in Michigan when we were introduced, and think I just told you how much I liked your reading. You had been sick and you were careful to rest a lot then. And then in New York this February with you in the hospital, I sat and talked and could already feel that there is another present time where you and I have been together for a long long time and here we continue together. In this place, in a sense, there never has been a time when you and I were not together. I cannot explain this. Maybe it is the continuing or on-going of the telling, the telling in poetry and stories.

Since the rains have come, the roadrunner is busy in other places, although he still roosts on the northwest side of the house, up on the roof.

After sundown the other night I was sitting on the road with Denny, and a great owl with eight-foot wings landed on a tall saguaro close to us. Jim, this owl was so big that, after he folded his wings, his size matched the diameter of the saguaro and he became part of the cactus top. It was only with the most careful concentration that I could see the owl swivel his head and thus believe that there was an owl sitting there. I thought about you then, Jim, as I always will when I am visited by the owls. He is probably the owl who carries off the cats the coyotes don't bother to catch, and after that night I was ready to believe this owl carries off whatever he damn well pleases.

It is so overwhelming to see your writing on the post card and to feel how much I miss your letters. There is no getting around this present time and place even when I feel you and I share this other present time and place.

Anyway, I treasure the words you write – your name most of all. But no matter if written words are seldom because we know, Jim, we know.

My love to you always,
Leslie

❦

New York, N.Y.
March 25, 1980

[To Leslie Silko:]

The best days are the first to go. The best of men has gone too.

Love,
Annie

ABOUT THE WRITERS

Leslie Marmon Silko is a Laguna Pueblo Indian, born in 1948. Her published work includes *Laguna Woman* (1974), *Ceremony* (1977) and *Storyteller* (1981). She recently received a five-year MacArthur Fellowship, and is currently on leave from the University of Arizona at Tucson.

James Wright was one of our most profoundly visionary poets. He was born in Martins Ferry, Ohio. He taught at the University of Minnesota, Macalester College and Hunter College. He was well known for his translations of Vallejo, Trakl and Neruda, as well as for his poems about the Midwest. His *Collected Poems* won the Pulitzer Prize in 1972. He died in 1980, at the age of 52.

The type is Fournier.
Designed by Tree Swenson.
Manufactured by Fairfield Graphics.